HOW TO COLLECT AND PROTECT WORKS OF ART

Night Welder, watercolor, E. Trick.

HOW TO
COLLECT AND PROTECT
WORKS OF ART

Harry A. Ezratty

OMNI ARTS
1988

Harry A. Ezratty
Copyright 1987

Cover design: José A. Peláez
Barbara Tasch, *Editor*

Omni Art, Inc., *Publishers*
Box 222
Stevensville, Maryland 21666

ISBN: 0-942929-02-0

LCCN: 88-090626

Dedication

*To Barbara, Laurie and Michelle, all of whom have taken
the step into the magic garden,
and to Philip Desind, who gave me the maps to the
best routes, on this journey I knew I had to take.*

Acknowledgements

A book such as this is impossible to create alone, simply because it is the sum total of learning from others over a span of years.

I thank every gallery owner who ever helped me understand collecting and how and where to seek, find and understand quality. I am indebted to every artist who patiently took the time to explain to me what he was doing, why he was doing it and the techniques he used to accomplish his or her dream.

To my wife, Barbara, for her professional help as my editor and for her consummate patience with me when our ideas about this book clashed.

To our friend, Selwyn Rosen, who took the photographs which appear in this book and fell in love with each work of art he shot.

To José Peláez, who besides pasting up this book, helped me to understand how to present it to readers so that they would enjoy the finished product.

Finally, to each and every artist for creating beautiful works of art that I loved enough to want to acquire for my collection. I do not own your wonderful dreams and creations; I am only their fortunate custodian during my lifetime.

Table of Contents

Introduction

This is a book for you, the beginner: for those of you who want to start collecting art either as a hobby or for profit. It's also a book for those who feel you simply "must" collect. This, too, is a book for people with limited amounts of money; for people who say, "I'd like to collect art, but it's too expensive." Or maybe you say "I don't know anything about art, so it's something I shouldn't spend money on."

Consider this: when I first began collecting art, 25 years ago, my average purchase for the first two or three years was between $35 and $150 for each item. Those same purchases today are worth from five to 500 times their original price.

Consider this: 25 years ago, most everyone's income was proportionately lower. Today's increased values of art, while real, also reflect inflation. Art may be priced higher than it was two and a half decades ago, but so is your income.

Also, there are more art galleries, more museums, more sources of information and more professionals willing to help a beginner today, by explaining, guiding, and leading the general public into the world of art, than at any other time in history.

This book is not intended to be a definitive treatise in art collecting. It does, however, cover the important areas a collector needs to be familiar with in order to get started. Every collector must then find his own road to building a personal collection. This book shows you how to get started, where to look, and what to look for.

If you were to ask me for a short capsule of what this book is about, it would be this: you needn't be wealthy to become an art collector. And you can learn about art through careful self-education.

There has never been a time when art was impossible to acquire by serious and dedicated collectors, but today, because there are more artists in the stream of commerce than ever before, collecting is easier than it has ever been before. So, if you're interested in art at all, you're living in its most prolific and exciting period. Today, you can select from dozens of styles and schools of art. You can pay astronomical prices for a canvas, or you can come home with a real bargain. It's up to you.

Read on, and get started.

Plate #1: *Cat's Paw*, engraving, Armin Landeck.

CHAPTER I

What to Collect

You see it all the time: long lines of people snaking around buildings in cities around the country. They're of all ages and lifestyles, judging from their varied dress... jeans, suits, dresses, shorts. Are they waiting to see the latest movie? No. A punk rock group? No. The building is a museum and the people are lined up to see an exhibit of paintings by an artist who has been dead over 100 years.

Twenty-five years ago, this exhibit would have attracted only a handful of dedicated art lovers and students. And fifty years ago, most artists fit romantic stereotypes: living in attics, barely making ends meet, working at odd jobs to buy paint and canvas. When they did occasionally sell their work, it was to selective collectors or the enlightened art gallery. Collecting art in those days was only for the wealthy.

But today, there are probably more art galleries, museums and collectors around than at any other time in history. Many things have caused the art explosion of recent years: the general public has more money available for collecting; the acceptance of multiple graphics has attracted a new group of collectors; the availability of reproductions has opened the door to art appreciation to the widest possible audience. Art has become big business. It can be purchased not only through galleries, but through catalogues, art auctions, and department stores, too.

Collecting art can be both a business and a gratifying way to express the creative side of your personality. Art beautifies your home and office as nothing else can. But before you begin to collect art, either as an investor or for personal pleasure, it's important to know how to look at it, how to understand it, and how to evaluate exactly what it is you are buying. You also have to know why you are paying that particular price for canvas or paper.

Having learned this process of selection—and you can—you will get pleasure from looking and acquiring. You will create a personal oasis in your home or office—a special place, stamped with your personality. If you're wise in your choices, your selections could increase in value, giving you a cash base for more buying.

Buying art is like any other capital investment: it can appreciate, depreciate or remain at the same price you paid for it. It depends on the current market.

Today, collectors can buy art at reasonable prices. The market is no longer limited to expensive oils and water colors. Now, there are affordable graphics which a collector can buy, either directly from the creator or through a gallery. Anyone can become a collector. It's simple. It requires application, a cultivated eye, and but little money.

Artists express themselves in many ways. Some paint on canvas or wood, using oil paints. That's called "oil," meaning it's created through the medium of oil-based paint. Oils are generally the more expensive works of art.

Artists also paint with water colors on paper, which can be less expensive to purchase.

Fine prints are another form of art. In a print, the artist creates his work on specially processed wood blocks, stones or metal plates. With these materials, he can make more than one copy of his creation, and run them off on special presses. Each copy is an original work of art. The artist may make 15, 30, or even 300 copies from a block, stone or plate. He usually numbers and signs each one after inspecting each carefully, to make sure that they meet his artistic standards.

Prints are popular because they are usually much less expensive than oils or water colors. When a well-known artist creates a print, you have an opportunity to buy his work at a lower price than it would cost to buy one of his original oils.

Artists also render drawings and sketches. These, too, can be wonderful bargains if you know how to go about buying them.

When you are known as a collector, people will seek your advice. In 25 years of art collecting, I have bought over 600 pieces of original art for myself and others. That's an average of

24 pieces a year: two works of art every month! I am not an art dealer, nor do I collect for profit. Yet people ask my opinion about pieces they want to buy, and my own collection has grown in value to the point where I must revise my insurance yearly to keep up with the collection's increased value.

Each time I buy a piece, I am filled with the same excitement and anticipation as I had with my first purchase. With each new acquisition, I cannot wait to frame the work, and hang it on the wall for my pleasure and the pleasure of others. When I make a choice based on my personal confidence and knowledge, it reinforces my excitement as a collector.

You, too, can feel the same way. These feelings are only some of the hallmarks of a real collector.

Anyone who collects art for pleasure, for profit, or for any other reason, must approach collecting systematically. To do otherwise would only cause aggravation, wasted money or even grief.

I had no art training at college, nor did I attend any art schools or adult education courses. I learned through my own interest and experience. You can, too. Some of the information I give you in this book I had to learn the hard way... it cost me extra time and money. Hopefully, my experiences can provide some positive information to other beginning collectors, and encourage you to get started.

When I began collecting, I had no spare cash. I was unsure of my tastes. So I bought photo-reproductions at $2 or $5 each, and hung them around my home and office. (Framing them cost more than the pictures.)

By constantly looking at these reproductions of famous works of art, and carefully selecting those which suited my personal tastes, I developed my own basic interests in art.

I also bought books and read everything I could about art. I went to museums regularly, and visited galleries to check both new artists and the output of the recognized masters. It took about three years before I had enough confidence to step into a gallery and make my first purchase, a small oil.

This leads us to the first decision you must make as a collector: What kind of art do you like?

There are many schools of art to choose from. Basically, they can be described as follows:

17

Representational Art creates scenes or objects which are reasonably identifiable. In other words, on a Representational canvas, a man, a cow or a building each look pretty much as we see them.

Within Representational Art, there are many variations:

Some artists paint canvasses that look like photographs: they are the *Photo Realists.*

Others paint with a realistic, three-dimensional perspective, known as *Trompe l'oeil*: objects which seem to leap out at you from the canvas.

Then, there are the *Impressionists*, who, while painting in a realistic fashion, use color or a changed perspective to alter what you are looking at. On close inspection, the canvas changes its look altogether.

Modern, or *Contemporary Art*, is another school, which includes *Cubism*. Picasso, Braque and Gris are the most reknowned early cubists.

Abstract Art is free-form: here, artists express themselves in mood, in movement, in form and in color. The canvas has different meanings to different observers. There is also *Color Art Field*... generally bands of color painted on canvas to create different effects when the colors come in contact with one another. Mark Rothko and Morris Louis are pioneers of Color Field painting..

Action Painting was made famous by Jackson Pollack. And there is *Abstract Impressionism* and *Surrealism*, which depict subjects as if in a dream. Dali and Magritte are the great practitioners of this form.

What I'm trying to say is this: there are many styles, or schools of painting. Many we have not even talked about. One or more of them should appeal to you, your personality, and your environment. How do you go about finding out which you like?

No matter where you live, there are museums, art galleries, and book shops nearby. Visit your nearest museum. Look at the works on exhibit. You'll soon find that you lean to a certain style of art over the others. You will find yourself skipping over some paintings to spend more time looking at canvasses that interest you more.

When you have discovered which type of art you enjoy, learn

everything you can about that school of art; its history, its development, and its leading practitioners, both past and present.

Museums sponsor art lectures, which you should attend. If your local museum has a lending service, you can get paintings on loan. I'll show you how to do that.

Visit the commercial art galleries in your community. You needn't worry about walking into one just to look, without buying. If a gallery is reputable, its owner won't mind you browsing. Your neighborhood bookshop or museum stocks art books. After you have discovered an art style that stimulates you, get books about the artists who are the leaders in that style. This will give you an idea of the work being done in that area.

Broaden your knowledge in every way that you can. Read your local newspaper's art section. Buy art magazines like "ARTnews," and subscribe to "The Print Collector's Newsletter." When you see art you like, make a note of the artist and the prices of his works. It's one of the ways you will get to know whether you are buying paintings at a good price, once you start buying.

You will also get to know and recognize artists within your field of interest. You will know the "stars" and the lesser lights. You will probably choose your own favorites, regardless of their professional standing. The important thing is that the choice will be yours after investigating, understanding, examining and cultivating your own unique taste.

A word about some other types of collecting. You may be interested in a particular subject, instead of a style. If your interest is in seascapes for example, you may choose to collect different styles of art on that one subject.

Or, you might choose to collect the works of one particular artist. Or one period of art. Or British, or French, or American art.

My advice is to collect within a certain theme, artist, period or subject. In the past few years, art collecting has become so specialized that it is practically impossible for the average collector to really understand each field and style. It is easier to concentrate in one area of special interest. In this way, you get to know what is happening in your area or field.

Plate #2: *Young Man*, charcoal, Robert Riggs.

CHAPTER II
A Glossary of Terms

An old Revivalist preacher in the South, trying to teach his congregation Bible lessons, said to them:

"First I'm gonna tell ya what I'm gonna tell ya.

Then I'm gonna tell ya.

Then I'm gonna tell ya what I told ya."

The old preacher instinctively knew that repetition was essential to get any message across. Most books put the glossary of terms at the end, almost as if it were an afterthought. I've reversed the order. I'm betting that if you take the time to read this chapter, the rest of the book will be more enjoyable.

I'll repeat information, but by the second time, it should have more meaning. So here are some of the terms used frequently in this book:

Aquatint: A type of color print used in connection with etchings or engraving. The colors appear as if they were water colors.

Artist's Proof: (also stated as A/P). Confusing category. The artists' proof is usually associated personally with the artist or may be his stamp of approval on a work as to the quality of the printing of a graphic work. Since neither of these criteria is actually followed by many artists today, the Artist's Proof has little meaning and is often abused by placing A/P on a print only to enhance its value.

Cancelled Plate: Any plate which has been used in multiple reproductions and then retired because the planned amount has been printed, either because it looses its brilliance due to wear, or because it is not intended to be reused. Cancellation is done by either defacing the plate or destroying it altogether.

Catalogue Raisonee: The compendium of an artist's works, with detailed descriptions and notes about them.

Cubism: The school of art which uses geometric forms to depict an object from any side and angle. The foremost founders and leaders of this school are Picasso, Braque and Gris.

Edition: The number of pictures pulled from a block or plate. This number may be extended by the number of Artist's Proofs produced.

Engraving: Any design cut into a metal plate, most often using a tool known as a burin.

Etching: Creating a design on a plate covered with wax. Acid is poured over the wax onto the exposed plate, etching the cut-through areas.

Fine Print: A term generally accepted amongst reputable dealers to define prints created by the artist, printed by him or someone under his personal supervision, and having the artist's final approval when printing is completed.

Foxing: One of paper's greatest enemies. It is a type of mold which grows on paper. It appears as a dark stain, brownish in color. Occasionally, foxing may cause small holes to form in the center of the stain.

Graphics: A general term defining prints of all types as opposed to oils, watercolors, drawings and pastels.

Impressionism: The school of painting which ascribes itself to reproducing the world through color. Impressionists believe that an object is never seen the same way twice, since light never strikes anything in exactly the same way more than once.

Lithograph: Any print created by means of a grease crayon drawn on a specially prepared stone or plate. Water is flushed over the stone, followed by greasy printing ink. Everything is rejected on printing, except for the design which the artist prepared.

Numbering: The practice of numbering prints is recent in art history and is done to apprise the collector of the amount of copies produced by the artist. Numbering has a bearing on value, since the fewer there are of a work, the scarcer it is and hence, the greater its value.

Pastels: A medium of powder held together by gum arabic. Pastels usually come in the form of sticks, which when drawn on paper, create a fine, chalky patina.

Oil: A popular medium of creating art, using ground pigment mixed with an oil base. Oils are the artist's most often used media and the medium most recognized by the general public as "art."

Ragboard: Also known as *Museum* or *Ph Board.* It is made of 100% rag. It is manufactured free of any harmful acids, and when used as a matting for watercolors, prints, drawings or pastels, will not affect the work of art through the contact of paper upon paper.

Serigraph: The method of making graphic prints through a silk screen and stencil.

Tempera: A method of painting using the yolk or white of an egg. The paint has great luminosity and strength.

Watercolor: Translucent colors, using water as a medium, and usually painted on specially processed paper.

Plate #3: *Whirpool*, engraving, James McNulty.

CHAPTER III
How to Look

Before the invention of the camera, buying and acquiring art was limited to the nobility, the church and the wealthy. They commissioned artists to paint a good likeness or a religious theme.

In those days, the great artists were those who could render scenes as close to reality as possible. They were portrait painters like Holbein, Durer, Velázquez, Van Dyck, Da Vinci, and El Greco. Artists were on retainer to the Church or one of the royal houses. They often lived with their sponsors, and were under no immediate financial pressure, except that they were obliged to produce acceptable works of art on a regular basis.

The finished canvas was the photograph album of the 17th century. Families were painted in groups, surrounded by their pets. The ancestral home was also often depicted. Religious themes were painted on church walls to stimulate parishoners.

In his "Lives of the Artists," Vasari, the 16th Century artist and writer, detailed the lives of some of the great Italian artists. Correggio, typical of them, is depicted as painting frescos for churches and the local nobility. Leonardo also worked for many Italian nobles and received commissions from the Church. One of his most famous paintings, "The Last Supper", was painted in Milan for the Cathedral of Maria Delle Grazie.

Rembrandt's *Night Watch* was originally commissioned by a Dutch Town Council and is a portrait of all of its members at one of their meetings.

During the 18th and 19th Century, itinerant artists roamed the English and American countrysides. They performed a service by offering to paint portraits of farmers, merchants and their families at reasonable prices. These men were called "Limners."

When the camera came along, that kind of art was no longer needed. Everyone could afford photographs of themselves. Still later, portable and less expensive cameras put everyone in the position of having the ability to photograph anything an artist could paint... and do it cheaper.

At first, the artists of the day tried to compete with the camera. It was a contest they could not win. Then, the artists turned to interpreting the world instead of duplicating it, by dealing differently with color, perspective, and form. They forced the observer to work when looking at a painting. They made the eye react to two carefully chosen colors placed next to one another, creating the illusion of seeing a third color which had not been painted on the canvas. Perspective was altered so that tables or roads were seen differently when observed from different angles of a canvas. This was called "Impressionism." The name came from Monet's painting of the Thames River called *Impression: Rising Sun.*

Next, artists broke form down into cubes. This is the school that Picasso, Braque and Gris founded. Then, form disappeared completely (in the sense we understand it, as a recognizable and identifiable representation of an object.) Artists began painting freely, blending colors and the actions of their minds and souls with free form. Collage—pasting strips of paper, rope or other objects on canvas—became a new and acceptable form of art.

Today, we have come full circle. Photo-Realists paint their subjects through a camera's eye, as if the canvas were a photograph. Artists again paint representational forms, but with a twist. Pop Art is representational: its practitioners, Andy Warhol, Tom Wesselman and Roy Lichtenstein mimic comic strip art as well as our popular culture.

Art's great geniuses have always departed from prevailing standards. Their works are timeless. This is what you must learn to look for when you begin collecting. Avoid fads and current "standards." A good artist is innovative and does not fear departing from the ordinary.

In later life, Rembrandt was denied profitable commissions, lost favor in the art world, and suffered financial problems, because he refused to paint according to the current standards. And because he insisted on painting as he felt, Rembrandt's genius bursts forth from his paintings. He creates light and reflections on gold, silver and metal beautifully. Shafts of sun and lamplight cross his canvasses as if someone had just opened a door from a sunlit street into a dark room. He treats wisps of grey hair on the elderly with reverent and supreme attention. Not until the Impressionists began painting and interpreting light some 200 years later do we again see such treatment.

Turner, the great 19th Century English painter, was painting in the Impressionist style 50 years before the French Impressionists began their experiments. A Turner painting is an experience in emotion. Nature: clouds, smoke, rain, fire and hail are all captured on the canvas. It is as if Turner had imprisoned them all behind a glass. Look carefully through all the swirling turbulence and haze. You may see the form of a ship, or a building, or deer grazing by a lake.

Turner tied himself to a ship's mast during a storm, and stuck his head out of a moving train in a thunder squall, to experience the feelings of those moments. In this way, he was able to put his feelings on canvas, to recreate his experiences. Yet his early paintings are pedestrian landscapes and seascapes, mountaintops and classic Greek buildings: the boilerplates turned out by every 19th century artist.

Rembrandt, Turner and others turned away from conventional standards to give life to their genius. This is what makes a great artist. It is one of the basics of good art. Great art is timeless, regardless of subject. A well-executed 17th century portrait, meant to be hung in a castle, is still good art hundreds of years later, if it is an artist's true expression. I need only to mention Da Vinci's *Mona Lisa,* or any Holbein or Durer portrait.

When artists turned from portraits and religious themes, to paint everyday life, their works became available to others beside the wealthy. It was still something only "cultured" persons acquired, but more people were becoming aware of art... and buying it.

At first, painters who varied from centuries of academic tradition were ignored. Impressionists took their easels outdoors and painted directly from nature. They learned an important fact: the sun never shines exactly the same way on anything from day to day or season to season.

Monet, Pizzaro and Van Gogh were ridiculed as bizarre and perverse. Monet, when he had some of his drawings examined by a famous art teacher, recalls being criticized for painting the model as he actually was. "That is ugly," said the teacher. "Don't follow nature," was the advice, "paint with style."

Impressionists painted the edges of their mountains and buildings fuzzy and soft. Their critics pointed out that everyone knew a cow was brown or black and white: using red and violet and yellow to portray a cow did not make sense. And they said that since nature did not make a cow that way, neither should man.

The truth is that before the Impressionists, the classical artists rarely, if ever, painted outdoors. As a result, those landscapes lack nature's real colors and dazzling reflections of light.

Impressionists often found it difficult to exhibit their paintings. Selling them was even harder. In 1894, Tanguy, the art dealer who befriended many of the Impressionists, died. His widow sold canvasses by Monet, Cezanne, Seurat and Van Gogh for what was even then absurdly low prices. Twenty-five years after the movement had started, Impressionist art was still not selling.

Impressionists experimented and experimented: in color, in form and in design. The adventure they set out upon over 100 years ago is still vibrant today, for Impressionism gave birth to Cubism. Once artists were no longer bound by the traditions of reproducing objects as they appeared, but could paint them as they felt them to be, Abstract and Modern Art followed.

What does this mean to you... a person who wants to collect art? There is much to learn about art before you begin to buy. Knowing something of art history is important, so that you may understand what today's artist is doing in relation to art's past.

How do you get started? At local museums. Become acquainted with their permanent exhibits, then the rotating ones. But what do you look for? "How can I tell good art from bad art?" you may ask. All art strives to achieve an effect. Bad art fails. Good art succeeds.

If an artist wishes to paint the North Pole, he will not use colors which are "hot": red, yellows and oranges. He will use colors that evoke the cold Arctic... the "cool" colors: blue and acqua. The artist may move you with the colors he uses, seeking to put you in the picture. He also wants to grasp your attention, to catch your eye. He does this by creating a central figure or design and having subsidiary parts of his canvas direct themselves toward what he wants you see.

How the artist does this is quite involved. For example, a landscape may show a meadow, clouds, sky and perhaps some hills in the background. If the artist wants to direct your attention to the meadow, he will paint angles in the hills and clouds and sky, all pointing toward the meadow. He can also do this by contrasting color on the least important parts of the canvas. He can divide his canvas in such a way as to dramatize the meadow. The artist can also use shapes to act as his pointer, or even letters of the alphabet cleverly hidden but apparent enough to create a desired effect.

Our response to color is also an artist's concern. He must be careful to use the correct color and combinations of colors to evoke the proper response from the observer. We all react to color, and there are universal psychological values for colors which artists make use of.

Perspective, or quality of depth perception, is another important part of the painting. This puts you, as the observer, into a relationship with the painting. Distance and proximity must be handled by the artist to encourage you to experience the painting as he wants you to see it. If you eliminate perspective or depth, you then create a "primitive," or "naive" effect. The artist does this consciously, since he wants to evoke certain responses from his observer.

If you are diligent, you will soon begin to recognize these things and more, because I have not outlined everything you should look for in a painting. If you attend lectures, as suggested, and look carefully at the art around you, you will see other things of importance in paintings. This is why I urge you to go to exhibits and museums... to hone your eyes on the works around you.

A tip: Many museums have a loan service. They will let you take a work of art home for a month, or weeks, or some other time period. Check with your local museum to see if it has such a program. There may be a small fee or nominal charge for this service. Sometimes, you may be able to buy the painting you have on loan, and apply the loan charges toward the purchase price. It's a wonderful way to test your tastes. After a painting hangs in your home, living with you, you'll get to know and feel the wonder of fine art. You may form an attachment to the painting, or wonder what ever attracted you to it in the first place!

You don't stop with museums, however. Go to art galleries. There, you will see works by both established artists and artists still struggling to achieve fame. Museums tend to show artists who have already gained some degree of recognition. Galleries are willing to show unknowns... those they feel have the ability to become tomorrow's masters. You will get great satisfaction in watching an unknown artist paint his way up from gallery to museum. If you recognized his talent at the gallery, you have given yourself an important boost in self-confidence... which you'll need, as a collector.

Visit art exhibits in your church and neighborhood. Look at art critically. Soon, you'll notice new things about canvasses that are important to you. Find out which styles of art moves you the most. When you have found it, become involved with it. Now you will know what you like, what you want to buy.

Exploit your cultivated taste. Most art galleries specialize in specific schools of art. Find those which exhibit your favorites. Then visit those galleries. Get copies of their catalogues of current exhibits. File them away. You'll soon be able to compare the works of different artists, in your own home. You'll be able to check prices and to watch the climb or fall of artists whom you've seen on exhibit. Go to your public library. Borrow books and magazines on art. Soon, you will see the same names repeated. They are the artists who are generally held in good standing by critics and art commentators.

A word of caution: Art is a matter of taste. Art history is filled with men who command great fees for their work and praise from contemporary critics. Generations later, however, they may have been completely forgotten. On the other hand, there are those who struggled for a lifetime without ever having received praise: Van Gogh sold only one painting while he was alive (and that was to this brother, Theo) yet today his works are priceless and prized. After you have gained enough confidence to buy what you like you will be buying not because a

30

critic has praised an artist, but because you know and feel him to be good. Then, you are on your way to having a successful collection, because you understand what you are buying.

A good, reputable gallery will always help you in every way. A gallery owner will explain paintings and their history. If you have established a proper rapport with the gallery, you might be able to take a painting home on consignment. Galleries are flexible. A reputable gallery knows that a knowledgable collector, treated fairly, is its best customer, now and for the future. Take advantage of this fact. Let the gallery owner help you. After a while, the gallery might make sales to you on a payment plan. If you are known at a gallery and a piece in your favorite style comes in, they will call you before they exhibit it publicly. You have become a favored customer, so why not give you first choice?

Before you buy, learn. Educate yourself. Feel. Understand. You are working towards that big moment: your first acquisition.

Plate #4: *Woolworth Through the Arch*, engraving, Joseph Pennell.

CHAPTER IV
How Much to Spend? What to Buy?

If you have a limited budget, but a great interest in getting started on the adventure of collecting, money is an important factor.

Art does not fit into some of the usual rules of finance. Collectors, seeking a particular artist or a special piece, can elevate the price. Since there can be only one *Mona Lisa* by Da Vinci, or one *Three Musicians* by Picasso, you can easily understand that the bidding for these unique objects do not follow the rules of the stock market. If a corporation puts out a million shares of stock on the market, those shares will have equal value amongst themselves as they increase or decrease. But the unique painting, being one of a kind, is bid at the moment for a particular price under pressure.

An unusually high bid for a particular Van Gogh will not necessarily elevate all other Van Gogh's to that figure. The reason is obvious: the sophisticated bidder is bidding for a piece that has historical significance or an unusual quality of execution.

Individual works have great worth when esteemed by collectors. Prints which I bought eight and ten years ago for $50 to $75, which were executed by then relatively unknown artists, now sell for $500 or more. A decade ago, no one was interested in these artists, but the wheels of the cycle have turned and now collectors realize their worth.

The point I'm making is that you should not despair if the art market seems too heady for you. Don't get discouraged. Artists who are at the top today once struggled for recognition. Collectors—those who are serious and knowledgeable— understood what those artists were doing and made shrewd appraisals about their potential. These artists' works were purchased early and at a relatively low price. You can do the same today.

The fact is that the art market must constantly replenish itelf with young, promising talent. If you are not looking to make a "killing," but rather to collect what pleases your educated taste,you will be happy with your purchase from an unknown newcomer. If you're lucky, the piece will be worth more in a few years.

For those with limited finances, the best bet is to start with the purchase of a fine print. Any oil, even if it's the work of a struggling unknown, will cost more than a print by that same artist. A print, remember, is a multiple of the artist's work. There may be 50 or 100 available, so it sells for less than the one of a kind oil or water color.

Remember, too, that taste and education are necessary factors in any art purchase. And you need not be alone when you make your purchase. You can enlist the aid of gallery owners and museum employees. The next chapter shows you how to go about getting that help.

The beginner must determine exactly how much he can set aside for collecting. Then, check publications such as *ARTnews*, *The Print Collector's Newsletter* and *The New York Times*. The prices listed for your prints in those publications will steer you towards satisfying both your taste and your pocket. In addition, from this examination you will soon acquire a sense of the "going rates" for artists, subject matter and period.

Perhaps you cannot find what pleases you. There are many other places to find inexpensive, quality art. There are art cooperatives: group of artists who share advertising, rent and other expenses. These artists tend to be new and their work sells inexpensively. Street fairs are also occasionally good sources of quality work, which a knowledgeable collector might capture. There are also print clubs, run by reputable dealers who sometime permit you to apply a membership fee towards a purchase. Further benefits of club membership include the opportunity to pre-publication purchases at lower prices than offered to the general public. There are also club memberships available at reasonable fees at most museums.

Between the museums and the print clubs, you will receive

much material about art. In the beginning, you will look to satisfy your curiosity. Soon, you will want to acquire. You will buy a work of art. It's a natural process, like moth to flame, or to express it better, like bee to honey.

It is important to consider your limited budget. One of the advantages of collecting prints is that there are so many of them available. If an artist makes 150 "strikes" of a specific work, the piece may wind up in the hands of several different dealers. If you're receiving the print dealer's catalogues, you may find a variation in price among them, of up to $250 or $300, depending on the piece. You can make your purchase more knowledgeably.

A word or caution: one dealer's price may be cheaper than another's because his print is in a poorer condition. Satisfy yourself that this is not so before you buy at the lower price. For this reason, you should maintain a library of catalogues. The professional collectors do. It will do at least two things for you: show you the current differences in prices and detail the performance of a particular piece by an artist over the years.

Catalogues for oil paintings and watercolors can only show increases and decreases over the years, and the prices for comparable works. Even then, the comparison can never be exact, but only an approximation. For these reasons, the best advice I can give to a beginning collector with a limited budget, is to start by collecting prints.

Plate #5: *Central Park Night*, lithograph, Adolf Dehn.

CHAPTER V
Looking: Fine Prints

Remember, always keep looking and learning. Your education in art should never stop. New styles and new artists will always appear. Your taste may change. As your budget increases, you'll be able to acquire more art of higher quality. You must be ready for these changes.

Right now, your budget is limited. You have studied and looked around. You are confident. You want to buy something you like. As I've said, fine prints are your best bet. In recent years, fine prints have become increasingly popular. As more people collect art, the fine print, because it is a multiple product, satisfies an artist's need to sell and the collector's ability to buy inexpensively. It may take a week to paint an oil and the same week to prepare a Fine Print. When the oil is finished, only one person can buy it, but perhaps up to 300 people can purchase a copy of the print.

The term Fine Print, as used here, covers lithographs, etchings, serigraphs, woodcuts and even potato prints: all works painstakingly prepared by hand. The term "print" has a double meaning. It can mean a work created by any multiple process, whether by hand or mass production, (machine or photo reproduction) as well as hand work. I use the term "Fine Print" to distinguish the hand work from the machine or photo reproduction products. Unscrupulous dealers will try to confuse you, because the term "print" is interchangeable. They call the machine and photo reproductions, prints.

Fine prints are produced in many ways. Woodcuts, for example, are made by drawing a scene on a block of wood. The artist then cuts away the areas he doesn't want to show up, leaving the higher, uncut areas to be produced. He then inks the block, covers it with paper, and puts it through a press. The ink from the uncut portions transfers to the paper, reproducing the scene.

The artist can repeat this process many times. He may make errors during any one printing. Smudges, smears or the force of a heavy press which may crack the block or alter the height of the uncut portions, all change the quality of the print.

A serious artist is concerned about what he releases to the public. And a good printing workshop takes care that the product is the best one possible. An artist should check each sheet as it comes off the press.

Having done so, he numbers his work and signs his name to it, in pencil. This is his way of saying, "I have examined this piece. I believe it to be good. I would like to you to buy it."

The artists numbers his prints like this: 28/100. That means that he has made 100 prints and you are looking at number 28. If the artists signs, "A/P" it means that it is an artist's proof, supposedly better in quality than the others that came off the press.

Another type of Fine Print is the lithograph. In lithography, an artist draws a scene on stone or metal plate, with a greasy crayon. Then he mixes the greasy areas with water. The grease rejects the water, and greasy ink is then rolled on to the previously marked areas. Put through a press, the moistened ink transfers to paper.

Etchings and Engravings are produced by drawing on a metal plate or similar substance, covered with wax. After the wax is cut away, exposing the metal plate, acid is poured over the wax and eats through the exposed area. The wax is then removed, having protected the uncovered portions from the acid's bite. Mezzotints and Drypoint are included in this grouping.

Serigraph, or silk screen, is a mask with a cut design on it. It's like a stencil. Either an air gun or a brush is used to paint the design on paper beneath the screen box.

There are other ways to create Fine Prints. Those which I have mentioned are currently the most popular. Woodcuts have a certain strength and character to them. Etchings and engravings are delicate, with fine turns of lines, and distinctions in shading. Lithographs have power picked up by the stone's surface. Serigraphs lend themselves to bright colors and interesting shapes and design. Each form has its advantages and disadvantages.

Not every artist can work in the media of Fine Print. This is important to know. Many artists who have been successful with oils and watercolors have been disappointing with their prints. That is because the artist is not working with oil and canvas, but stone and wood and metal plates. Instead of using a brush, he is cutting with a knife or etching a waxed plate, or shooting an airgun through a cutout. Two famous artists who successfully made the transition from canvas to prints are Robert Rauschenberg and Robert Motherwell. Their prints are expensive, but widely sought by collectors.

Many artists work only in Fine Prints. Get to know them. The best of them produce treasures that would put sunshine in anyone's home. To mention them all would be to list hundreds of names. Keep looking and you will see the same artists at shows, winning prizes and being written about. If these artists move you, collect them.

Collecting Fine Prints can be complicated. There is much to know. And it's easy to be fooled. The first thing you must do when you go shopping for prints is to bring along a magnifying glass. Magnified, a photo-reproduction, which is not a Fine Print, shows up as a series of dots, forming light and dark areas to make a design, much as a photograph in a newspaper. You will not see such dots on Fine Prints.

Some artists will photo-reproduce work they did years before, and then sign and number them to give you the impression they are Fine Prints. Don't be fooled. Save your money. What you are buying is worthless. They are, however, also called prints, and as I've said, you can get confused and cheated if you are not wary.

Years ago, in Paris, a magazine published lithographs by Chagall. A London gallery clipped them out and then stamped his name onto the prints. Many people were fooled into thinking that they were original works by Chagall. Had they used a magnifying glass, they might have discovered the fraud.

The magnifying glass will also allow you to judge the quality of the work you are considering. In serigraphs, you may see an overlapping of colors, where the artist carelessly covered over one color with another.

You may also see smears and breaks. Perhaps it doesn't make a difference to you. You want the piece and those flaws aren't that important. Fine, but most times you'll want to know about those smudges and overlaps before you put out good cash. You can point out the flaws to the seller, to bargain for a lower price.

A magnifying glass can also show if there are small tears in the paper, or stains caused by age, water or fungus; all of these the great enemy of art. These defects have a bearing on the value of a Fine Print. With a magnifying glass, you can compare two or more prints of the same edition and see the differences. You may choose one over another because of shading or intensity of color. Each of these things have importance on the print's value.

Recently, in a California gallery, I saw a serigraph I wanted to purchase. The gallery's copy was defective. There were smudges and marks within the work, easily seen with a magnifying glass. I arranged with the gallery to send me a better copy through the mail, retaining the right to reject any subsequent copy for defects, or even to cancel the sale.

Several copies were sent. All proved to be defective under the glass. Finally despairing of getting a good print, I cancelled the sale. Months later, speaking with another dealer in New York, I discovered that the artist had sold the plate to someone, who then controlled the printing. Part of the agreement was that the artist was obliged to sign all of these prints, although he had lost control of his work. As a result, this particular piece was selling for less than half the price of his other works, which were well-produced because the artist had personally supervised their printing.

A word about numbering and signing. Historically, Fine Prints were neither numbered nor signed. That practice is relatively recent, and can be confusing if you are not aware of what numbering means.

An artist advertises that he has made 100 "strikes," or copies, of his prints. You are entitled to believe that only 100 copies are around. Depending upon the artist, however, he may make an additional four artists' proofs and may keep 10, 12, or more extra copies for himself, which aren't included in the numbering. This is important to know, because usually the more copies of a print there are, the lower its value.

When you buy a Fine Print, find out how many strikes there were, including Artists Proofs. A reputable workshop and artist will always reveal all facts about numbers. They wouldn't have it any other way. And don't let a dealer tell you the lower the number the better the quality. It isn't so. If the artist and the workshop have done their jobs well, all prints should be of equal quality. Artist's proofs, as we already said, means the artist especially approves of that one. Again, it has little meaning if they were all printed with care.

If an edition of a Fine Print is only four or five, they should be worth more than an edition of 100 of some other work by the same artist. My advice is not to buy any prints that exceed 200, unless the edition is by an outstanding artist. Even 200 is pushing it; you are approaching mass production.

If you are buying the work because you can't live without it, okay. But production in such numbers tends to lessen value. Conscious of that, if you still like the piece and must have it, go ahead: the question of numbers is relative.

Unfortunately, when you buy something, you have to establish a price. You want it to increase in value. A great artist's work will always sell. Artists like Ben Shahn and Thomas Hart Benton didn't like numbering their work so there are times when you must do some investigating to determine what you are buying.

I own some prints that are from editions of 15 or 30. They are worth many hundreds of dollars—even thousands—because there are just so many of them. I own Fine Prints of four strikes, that are individually hand-colored by the artist. They are worth more than other works in an edition of 200 put out by the same man. I also have a fine piece by Thomas Hart Benton. It's unnumbered. I'm sure it will always be worth at least what I paid for it.

You may often see works that have an odd number of strikes, such as 74 or 32. What has happened here, unless the artist actually planned that number, is that after printing that number, the quality began to change. The serious artist and the ethical workshop would then stop the run, without producing any more. Plates are usually destroyed after their run so that they may not be reproduced by others and also to insure the numbers as you bought them.

The paper an artist uses is important. Learn about it. I will discuss this at greater length in the chapter on the care of your art works. For now, you must consider that a Fine Print is a pigment divinely set down on paper. And paper is a delicate thing. So artists carefully select their paper to withstand the assaults of time and weather. This is why a print is mounted beneath glass: to seal it from the outside; from dust, humidity and dirt.

When you hold a Fine Print to inspect it, don't grasp it between your thumb and forefinger. You'll leave your fingerprints all over it. Your hands also have acids and salts on them, both of which are enemies of paper and capable of biting through its soft edges. Carefully pick up a print by its edges, and hold it by its back, with the back of your hand to the paper.

Take care not to crease a print. Check the type of paper on which the edition was issued. Fine printing papers, like Rives, Arches or Japan paper, have watermarks which you can see. These papers, and others of similar quality, are designed to last. Any work produced on cheap paper will have a relatively short life span.

I've already said that it's only recently that prints have been signed and numbered by artists. That's not the only difference between the older prints and the newer ones. Today, most artists will destroy or deface their plates, blocks, screens and stencils after they have made all their copies. Centuries ago, great artists like Rembrandt or Durer never destroyed their printing plates. Nor did they sign or number them. They scratched their names on the plates. That was enough. Consequently, and this may surprise you, you can still buy some Great Masters fairly reasonably. Museums have acquired the plates which have been refaced and, from time to time, they issue new editions. They do not, however, have the clarity and brilliance of the first sets that were struck. Nevertheless, they are "pulled" from the artist's original plates.

Original editions may be detected by certain burrs, or shading, in them. (Get your magnifying glass again.) Some art historians have devoted their careers to cataloging all the Fine Prints of particular artists. Such a work is called a Catalogue

Raisonee. These compilations are important and you should learn how to use them.

If you are planning to buy a print of one of the Masters of the 17th, 18th, or 19th century, proceed with caution. Their plates were often altered after their deaths, by other artists who acquired them. Of course, such alterations reduce value. But it doesn't stop some dealers from calling them "Rembrandts'" or "Durers'". Consult the Catalogue Raisonee before you buy. You might also consult with another dealer.

And, of course, bring your magnifying glass. Artists often make their own changes in their plates after they print several copies of a work. They move a cloud here, eliminate a mountain there. It's natural. Artists design for impact and effect. Moving shape around helps toward that end. These changes are called "states." It is important to know what state you are buying, because it has a bearing on cost, quality and desireability.

A Catalogue Raisonee is also important for other information. It tells you how many of an edition were printed, and which museums and public and private collections have copies. Armed with this type of information, it will be hard to fool you. If artist X printed 10 copies of a work, and 10 are in museums, you will be wary of any individual who claims to have such an edition for sale.

Private collections of importance use "provenances," or special markings, to show that a print came from a certain collection. Knowing this also helps you to authenticate a piece in which you may be interested. A provenance also adds a pedigree to a piece.

It's easier to establish the value of a Fine Print than a painting. Why? Because an edition may have 100 or 200 strikes, so they are frequently in the market place, unlike one oil on canvas.

How do you take advantage of this? Get on the mailing list of galleries that specialize in prints. You will get the current prices for prints. Keep up on the auction prices for prints. You will see the same prints showing up again and again. That's also a good indication of prices. If you plan to specialize in collecting prints, you should get monthly newsletters about prints. They have all sorts of information: sales price, auction prices and listings of galleries. That's what a professional does.

I've included a bibliography at the end of this book. It suggests books and periodicals that may help you to gather more knowledge and help you get maximum value for your money.

Once you know what to pay for a Fine Print, check it carefully. The price may vary according to its condition (get your magnifying glass out again.) Any deterioration, stain, or tear on a Fine Print reduces its value. At this point, you have to determine how much the defect will lower the price, and how badly you want the piece for your collection.

One woodcut I bought several years ago for $75 was recently shown in a exhibit. Its selling price was $450. When the gallery exhibit ended, it was featured in the next exhibit at the same gallery 10 days later... for $750! I've seen prices rise, but never so quickly for this kind of work.

On my next visit to the gallery, I mentioned my suprise at the $300 jump for one exhibit to another, within 10 days. "They're not the same print," explained the gallery salesman. "The $450 print shows a crack in it, in the shape of a cross. It's from a broken plate. It's very definite, you can't miss it. The $750 version is clean... no cracks." I checked my edition when I returned home. Fortunately, my copy of the print had no cracks. I had a clean one.

You can always bargain for a print and try to get it at a lower price. That's part of the fun of collecting, the hunt: Tracking down what you want and getting it at your price. And prices do vary.

In New York City, I once bought a Fine Print that was a part of a gallery's show of a particular artist. I loved the piece, and paid $450 for it. I felt it was high, but there were only 30 strikes, it had been printed during the Depression, and the artist had been dead for several years. A day later, I was in Washington, D.C. and saw the same print in a gallery window for $300. I promptly bought it and returned the other one, saving $150.

This leads to another thought, another lesson: the Fine Print I just described was a scene of New York City. Since the artist, scene and place of purchase were all of New York City, that increased the price. Such a combination would not command the same price in Washington, D.C.

Conversely, an artist who is well known in California, or

New Mexico, would command more money in his home territory than out of it. So, if you are fond of a particular artist, or a particular sectional scene, try to find the work away from its home. You may save yourself a lot of money. Of course, national and international artists don't fit into these rules. Their works command similar prices wherever they are found.

One further word: two decades ago, I was buying works by artists few people had ever heard of. Their prints were sold by a brave band of devoted print collectors who sold to an equally brave group of collectors. Over the years, the artists have become more familiar and more important. Now, hardly a catalogue, auction or exhibit passes by without one copy of the prints I purchased not so long ago. Such events can give not only confidence to the collector, but punctuate a belief in a cultivated taste.

Plate #6: *Trio at Luchows*, oil on board, Frank Ashley.

CHAPTER VI
Looking: Oils and Watercolors

Whenever most people think of art, or artists, they conjure up scenes of someone standing before an easel, palette in hand, dabbing a canvas with oil paints.

The fact is that after many centuries, oils are still the most popular and versatile medium for artists. More can be done with canvas and oil than with any other forms of art. For one thing, an artist can paint large canvasses, 10 to 20 feet in length, in oil—something that is quite difficult, if not impractical, with fine prints or watercolors. Colors of different shades and tones can be mixed and then painted over if the artist wants to make a fresh start.

An oil painting is not as delicate and fragile as a fine print on paper. Oils need care, but they are more durable than the inks and colors used in fine prints or the pigments of watercolors.

Artists have not always used oils. Supposedly, Jan van Eyck, a Dutch painter, discovered its use in the early 1400's, but actually there is proof of the use of oils before that. However, once discovered, oils were widely used.

Aside from knowing how to design a work of art, artists until fairly recently also had to make their own paints. They did this by grinding pigments into oil. Occasionally, they would add egg for a tough glaze called Tempera. Every artist had his own secrets for the preparation of his paints. Some added wax; others, glue.

The artist even made his own canvas. The early artists not only knew how to paint, but also knew the art of preparing his working materials. In his book, *Painter's Progress*, Maurice Grosser details the successes and frustrations of a 20th century painter, in his quest to make his own paints and canvasses.

Paints improperly prepared or dried can crack or quickly deteriorate and shred from mildew, fungus or other rot.

As I've said before, oil paintings are generally more expensive than fine prints. They are, if you care to look at it that way, custom made. One of a kind. Unique. The price of an oil painting depends on several other factors, as well. Who is the artist? At what stage in his career was this canvas painted? Is this piece one of his representative works at his peak? Is this artist dead or alive? Can we authenticate the painting?

We should consider all of this separately. Who is the artist? If he is famous in the history of art, a painter such as Picasso, Monet, Van Dyck or Carvaggio, his works will be priceless, and probably out of the price range most of us can afford. We must be satisfied to see his work at museums, mansions or galleries.

At the other extreme, if the artist is unknown, you will be able to buy his work cheaply. Every large city has art shops which sell bargain-priced oil paintings in the same way you would buy detergent at the supermarket. The prices range from $5 or $15 to $200 or so. Most of this type of art is worthless from a collector's standpoint. Once in a while, you might come across a well-executed piece that is worthy of your consideration. But generally, that kind of shop offers very little for the collector, who should never consider buying a painting because it "matches" a couch or a rug, or goes well on a certain wall. Chances are such a purchase will prove to be a mistake.

Getting back to who the artist is: if you have been careful about looking and investigating, you will know about the artist when you buy his oil. Acquiring an oil is usually a relatively large investment, so you should consider its creator. One good way of determining the artist's standing is to know where he has exhibited before and which museums and private collections have acquired his work.

For example, by now you have learned that in addition to galleries, museums also specialize in what they show and collect. If you are looking at American abstract painters whose works have been acquired by the Whitney Museum in New York City (they specialize in Modern or Contemporary American artists) you can be sure that his work is a quality representation of the style in which he is painting. Major museums are careful when giving their imprimateur, or stamp of approval, to an artist by acquiring or exhibiting his works.

Get to know the specialities of the major museums and private collectors. Wealthy private collectors hire professionals to manage their collections. You may be guided by their tastes, but don't be a slave to them. Don't fall into the trap of paying for an artist because he has suddenly been acquired by a museum or a major private collector. Learn to say, "Thanks, but no thanks," unless you are collecting for profit only. It can be risky to buy that way. Besides, we both know your budget is limited.

Our next consideration is: at what state in the artist's career was the work created? This is important. Franz Kline, the American painter, began his career doing some fine representational art. Later, with his friend Jackson Pollock, he broadened his field and began doing abstractions, experimenting with black color in broad slashes across his canvas. The abstract works are what Kline collectors look for. While his representational pieces are excellent, they do not sell for the same price as his later works.

Conversely, Thomas Hart Benton, the epitome of Representational art in America, studied in Paris as a young man. He succumbed to the influence of the abstract painters and did several such canvasses. When he returned to America, he "repented," and began painting representationally. No serious Benton collector, who collects his work because of his style and the statements he makes, would consider buying these abstract paintings. These would have historical interest, but are not representative of Benton's life work.

Is the piece you are looking at one of the artist's representative works at his peak? Artists are like you and me. They have good days and bad days. They have fruitful periods and arid periods. In good times, they paint some of their best canvasses. At other times, they seem to push out what is, for them, mediocre. Of course, this influences the value of the piece. It is important for you to know that even the most wonderful artists are capable of turning out what is, for them, substandard work. When you are buying an oil by a well known artist, don't just buy the name. Make sure you buy the quality with which the name is associated.

Many times, famous artists who can produce great works

turn commercial. They sell their names, usually in fine prints. But the public, captivated with the name, pays high prices for slap-dash art.

Collectors are often faced with having to select one canvas from two or three by the same artist. You may make a selection on the basis of what you want to spend. My advice is this: Unless the price is an overriding consideration, buy the best of the group. You'll never regret your choice.

Is the artist dead or alive? Perhaps you are going to tell me, "if an artist is dead, his paintings are worth more." Not necessarily so. Art styles and artists' popularity are subject to cyclical variations, as everything else in this world. Works of dead artists, such as Van Gogh, Michelangelo or Da Vinci are priceless museum pieces, which neither you nor I can touch. Should an artist die at the peak of his artistic powers, riding the crest of an art style, that will probably cause his price to rise. Whether prices remain high, however, only time can tell. Often, when an artist dies, he becomes forgotten.

Currently, artists who were popular at the turn of the century and then forgotten, are being revived. A few years ago, their oils could have been bought for a few hundred dollars. They now command prices of thousands upon thousands. Because the art is good? I cannot say. Someone riding a fad in a style? Perhaps. One man bought up all of the art of a certain turn-of-the-century style he could find, got some publicity and then got out by selling the whole collection for a fortune.

Two American artists who were generally unknown during their lifetimes have recently enjoyed much deserved attention. They are Arthur Dove and Charles Burchfield. Both men painted during the Depression and into the 1940's and 1950's, in highly personal styles. Dove turned to farming to earn a living, but kept on painting. Burchfield, after trying New York, returned to Ohio to paint his fabulous visions of Gothic houses which came alive on stormy nights.

Neither man had a following, or was responsible for founding a school of art, but today, decades after their deaths, their works are still fresh, original and timeless. Neither Burchfield nor Dove will ever paint again, of course. The public, having discovered them after their death, has only so much product to buy. The demand far exceeds the supply.

Today, there are hundreds of thousands of artists painting. Some paint full time, earning their living from their art. Others paint part time, without selling any of their work, or at best, selling very little. Artists no longer need commissions or patrons in order to survive, as they did centuries ago. Anyone can buy commercial paint and canvas today, rather than having to make the paint and canvas as they did centuries ago. Then, if an artist didn't have a commission or a patron, he couldn't find anyone to sell his work to. Now, there are many buyers in the market place and competiton is keen. There are many artists out there, toiling unrecognized because they don't have the business skills necessary to publicize their works. Some don't know how to market or are painting in a style that no one wants. If you are fortunate and informed, you may discover such an artist, who is, nevertheless, worthwhile.

Can we authenticate the painting? Art forgery is a big business. Of course, forgers are not troubling to fake unknown artists, but our times are full of enchanting rascals who have made fortunes expertly duplicating well-known painters. You must check carefully, and track down the painter's pedigree. If the artist is alive, he's the one to verify the canvas.

There is a story, apocryphal perhaps but it serves to make a point: A famous writer once bought a Picasso oil at a gallery. He hung it in his home. After he'd had it for a while, a knowledgeable collector came by and saw the painting on the wall. "It's a fake," he said. "That's no Picasso!"

The writer happened to know Picasso. He put the canvas under his arm and went to the great man's house. "I bought this several weeks ago, and now they tell me it's a forgery," he said. Picasso picked up the painting, examined it closely by the light of his window, and placed it on his easel. With his brush, he made a series of strokes. He turned to the writer, smiled, and said, "My friend, now you have a genuine Picasso."

Generally, as you have read, there are many variables that enter into the value of a painting. We've discussed some of the more important ones. There are always others, including personal considerations. You may need a particular painting to round out your collection, or you may find that you cannot live without a certain piece; you must have that painting at all costs. One of the signs of an avid collector is that if he wants a painting, he will somehow manage to acquire it, regardless of the obstacles.

My personal yardstick is that if I want a piece of art, I acquire it immediately. Or arrange to tie it up for the future by putting a deposit on it. Too often, I've left works behind, thinking I'd buy them the next time around. They weren't available the next time around. You must determine for yourself how to react under such conditions.

Once, I bought a watercolor at a gallery. While I was still there, a couple walked in and saw what I'd just bought. "Oh," said the husband, "I've been looking at that for a few months. I really want it." He then offered me something more than what I had just paid for it. I refused because I liked the picture as much, if not more, than he did. He gave me his name and address, saying "Contact me if you want to sell it." I still own the piece.

The same considerations that go into fixing the price of oils are applicable to watercolors. Keep in mind, however, that some artists are well known as watercolorists, which adds to the value of their work. If an artist is famous only as a printmaker, or an oil painter, you might have a bargaining point when acquiring his water color.

Watercolor is a medium which, because of its transparent and luminous qualities, has great charm. This a difficult medium to work in. The artist usually cannot correct mistakes. He often works in a rapid, abbreviated manner. Some of America's finest artists were experts with watercolor. Winslow Homer, John Marin and Charles Burchfield have brought watercolor to its height.

Plate #7: *Greetings from the Weyhe*, woodblock, Howard Cook.

CHAPTER VII
Hidden Treasures: The Artist's Studio and the Early Visit to the Gallery

In order to become a knowledgeable collector, you must learn to work with art dealers who handle the styles, works and artists you favor. Good art dealers can spot a promising artist years in advance. Good art dealers instinctively know quality despite current trends; good art dealers will understand your economic limitations and work with you to help you buy within your budget.

I've been fortunate to have met and learned from some wonderful dealers... people who love their work and would never direct a client down the wrong path.

Here are some of the galleries with which I have dealt over the years. They have different approaches to selling, but all have two things in common: they are helpful and they take the time to explain.

Each of these galleries deal in, among other works of art, my personal collecting tastes, that is, American representational art of the Depression years. In addition to the galleries I mention here, you should develop your own set of dealers and establish your own relationships with them.

While these galleries might not be close to where you live, almost all of them have catalogues and send announcements of their exhibits. Most of them would be pleased to put you on their mailing list and sell to you through the mail.

Capricorn Galleries, 4849 Rugby Ave., Betheseda, Maryland:
This place is fantastic. Owner Philip Desind hangs less than 5% of his paintings on his gallery's walls. The rest are stacked in what appears to be a haphazard manner throughout three rooms. Serious collector or neophyte, you are obliged to go

through hundreds of oils, water colors, drawings, pastels and acrylics. Each flip of a stacked, framed painting will reveal a gem you might covet. On tables are watercolors, unframed in mats. Then, there are works squirreled away in drawers.

My first contact with serious collecting began here 25 years ago. Many of the truly good things I bought at Capricorn were discovered at the botton of a pile, in a seemingly forgotten corner, or hidden in one of the many drawers lining the walls.

Capricorn has at one time or another handled many of the great American representational artists at truly reasonable prices. Desind has an uncanny ability to recognize and predict "stardom quality" in an artist. His personal collection is awesome and a tribute to his knowledge as a collector.

E. Weyhe, 794 Lexington Ave., New York City

In the heart of Manhattan, between 61st and 62nd Streets, Weyhe is soul food for the true collector. The gallery has been at this spot for a long time and its walls give you a feeling of tradition.

You climb the stairs to the flight above the street level book shop (which is also part of the Weyhe) and step into one large room lined with table stalls filled with matted prints carefully covered with protective plastic. Although Weyhe deals basically in fine prints, you will, as you go from table to table, uncover water colors, pastels and even oils.

The Wehye carries many major American printmakers, but you will also discover works of other artists from other countries. Whenever I go to the Weyhe, I'm always sure I know how print collector sought their treasures so long ago—in stalls instead of bins or rotating plastic sleeves.

Newmark Gallery, 1194 3rd Avenue, NYC

Partners Carlos Pacheco and Tony Graham have created a gem of a gallery, exhibiting art works from Japanese and Italian mezzotints to oils by European artists.

If you seek integrity in your dealer, you'll find it here. We first discovered this gallery 6 years ago when we sought the print of a certain artist. Carlos Pacheco refused to sell us the work because he knew it to be of inferior quality and he so advised us. That began the relationship of dealer-client and a personal friendship that I treasure.

It is here that I first learned of Fred Mershimer, who is steadily gaining stature as a major American printmaker.

When I step into Newmark, I usually find Carlos and Tony explaining the painstaking technique of mezzotints, engravings or lithographs. They genuinely want their clients to understand what they are buying.

Associated American Artists, 20 West 57th Street, NYC

Practically the grand-daddy of American printmaking, this gallery issued works of such greats as Thomas Hart Benton, Louis Lozowick, Howard Cook and Reginald Marsh for $5, $10 and $15 during the difficult Depression years.

AAA sells only prints. If you can't find something for your tastes here, you're hard to please. At the AAA, you'll thumb through every style of art in color or black and white, lithographs, engravings, seriographs, woodblocks and mezzotints. You'll find old prints, new prints, traditional and experimental works.

What I like about AAA is that it carries up and coming artists, stocks noteworthy Americans of the past 100 years, and world masters such as Rembrandt, Durer and Daumier. Visit the gallery to get the feel of its scope.

Other Galleries: At one time or another, I've purchased works from galleries in San Francisco, Los Angeles, Scottsdale, New Orleans, Miami, Atlanta and Boston, among others. Here are some I've dealt with more than once, that you might want to investigate:

Craig Flinner, N. Charles St., Baltimore, Md.
Sylvan Cole Gallery, 101 W. 57 St., New York City
Marylin Pink, 817 N. La Cienaga Blvd., Los Angeles, Ca.
Nahan Galleries, 3000 Magazine St., New Orleans, La.

A few galleries I've dealt with over the years have closed shop. When that happens, it's like saying goodbye to old friends. But then, you should being looking around for new ones.

So much attention is paid to fine prints, watercolors and oils that the relatively forgotten area of drawings, sketches and pastels can be your treasure trove. While everyone else is tracking down the more popular types of art, you may find less competiton for drawings and sketches.

Someone once said, "Drawings are to art what chamber music is to music." Drawing is artistic shorthand: it is a way of expressing ideas with pencil, charcoal or pastel. The artist works economically; one line expressing several characteristics. Most artists have done some drawing during their careers.

I have been telling you to go to art galleries, museums and bookshops, and lectures. What you should also do is go to the artist's studio in your quest for drawings and sketches. When you have the opportunity to meet artists, try to arrange to go to their workshops. I guarantee you will find treasures you've never dreamed of. Artists are never more pleased than when they meet someone who is genuinely interested in their work. Don't feign pleasure with an artist's work if you really don't like it. He will know you are just trying to be pleasant. If you are sincere, however, most artists will be happy to invite you to see the place where they create their work.

In an artist's studio, you will see all sorts of things: the paintings he has not sold; the paintings he's sold that are waiting to be picked up; the things he is working on at present; and the material he is gathering for his current exhibit. You can really get a good idea of the artist's total production by seeing all of these works at once. Aside from this, you will also see sketches, drawings and layouts; the preparatory material an artist creates before he paints his final canvas.

I once visited an artist in his loft in New York City. I liked his work very much, but couldn't buy any of his oils. They were huge, six feet by six feet and larger. He saw that I was genuinely interested in his work, so he went to a bin where he kept his drawings and prints. Obviously, it was the neglected corner of his studio.

"There might be some things here you'd like," he suggested. What he kept in that bin were absolute gems! I bought a lovely pencil drawing of a nude, and a lithograph the artist had done years before but had never put up for sale. I acquired them at bargain prices. The artist is well known. The Federal government commissioned him to do a painting for the Bi-centennial

Plate #8: *El Conde*, pencil sketch, Samuel Lind.

celebration, which together with works of other well-known artists, was shown around the country.

On another occasion, I visited the California studio of an artist I had admired for years. I never bought any of his paintings, because his canvasses were also large. It took him as much as six months to complete one. This put his work out of my reach financially, but did not stop me from following his career. I was always aware of the new works he was producing.

To my suprise and delight, when I arrived at his studio, he was finishing a small (12" x 10") painting of his grandfather. I fell in love with it, but he would not sell it to me because of a previous commitment with his dealer-representative. I knew the dealer, and when I returned East a week later, I made a bid for the painting. I would never have had the opportunity to buy it otherwise. This artist is in such demand that as soon as collectors know one of his works has arrived at the gallery, it is snapped up.

Again in California, I stumbled on an artist's studio by erroneously believing it to be a public gallery. The artist, well known and popular, was delighted to see one of his "fans." I stayed for several hours, learned that we had grown up only a few blocks from one another, and left with half a dozen prints at substantially reduced prices. But best of all, I made a friend of an artist I had long admired.

When an artist knows you are interested in his work, he will show you whatever he has. It's common sense. An artist needs to know his work is appreciated. If you show an interest, he'll explain his work to you. What better way to learn about style than directly from the artist!

A tip: Many artists do preliminary sketches, drawings and black or white or color studies of their major oils. The studies are often discarded in a corner. Hunt them out! The only way you can do that is to go up to the studios. I admire a young and talented artist in Puerto Rico, who generally sells his oils even before they're finished. I've never been able to acquire one. But a trip to his studio resulted in my buying two delightful pencil sketches for one of his major works.

Artists do not usually think much of their preliminary sketches. They see them as rough steps to the final painting to which they have been devoting their time and energy. You may be able to buy these studies from the artist at good prices. If you should buy an oil painting directly from the artist, he may throw in accompanying studies as part of a whole package.

A word about galleries. When one of your favorites galleries is going to have a show of an artist in whom you are interested, visit the gallery before they mount the show. You will have the chance to see the whole show before the general public does. If you see something you want, buy it. The gallery will hold the painting until the show is over. Your purchase will sport a red dot on its frame, to show everyone that it's off limits, already sold.

Galleries are not just public exhibiting rooms. The back of galleries are jammed with hundreds of works. Gallery owners can't hang everything they own; there just isn't enough space. Ferret around in the back room. You'll be surprised at what you find. It's like the artist's studio. Even better, because there's so much of so many artists. The gallery is in business to sell artists' works for a profit. It's always a good day for any gallery when they can sell a work not publicly exhibited.

Plate #9: *Erie Railroad Yards*, lithograph, Reginald Marsh.

CHAPTER VIII
Seek and Find: Auctions and Attics

Galleries and artists are the main sources of art. But there are others. One fine and popular outlet is the art auction. And you should also learn to look in attics, antique shops, and just plain junk shops.

Attics are a wonderful source of supply. Many people forget or simply do not realize what they have in their attics. No wonder. The stuff gets carried along from generation to generation, building up until the bottom layers are covered over and lost to sight. If you have studied and know what to look for, attics can be one of your biggest sources.

A few years ago, the state of New Jersey held an exhibit of paintings pulled out of attics along the New Jersey countryside. The art found hidden away was important, and of well-known artists. That's proof that if you can rummage through attics, and know what you're looking for, the results may astound you.

Recently, I visited an attorney in his office in St. Thomas, U.S. Virgin Islands. When I walked in, I was immediately taken by a large painting of a trailer camp, hanging in the office. The style was familiar and the painting had obviously been done by a professional. The lawyer stepped out for a moment, leaving me alone. I had the opportuinty to walk up to the canvas and look at the artist's signature. It was Steven Dohanos. It was unusual to see such an artist (Dohanos is a famous magazine illustrator) painting in the Caribbean, but then I remembered that during the Depression he, like so many other artists, had painted murals in Federal buildings for the W.P.A. Dohanos had done one for the St. Thomas post office.

When the lawyer came back, I asked him about the painting. "Oh," he said, smiling, "it's not mine. It's a loan. When Dohanos lived in St. Thomas, he was befriended by a family I know. He gave them the painting, which was used as a *Saturday Evening Post* cover. When I first saw it, it was stuck away in a corner. The family lent it to me, I framed it, and it's now the way you see it."

Sometimes you read in newspapers of finds worth millions of dollars. They are unusual. That's why they make news. A collector I know bought two small medieval portraits from a returning soldier right after World War II. Thinking they were of little value, he hung them in his home along the staircase leading to the upper floor. Several years later, in a book about stolen art treasures, he recognized his two miniatures as priceless Albrecht Durers' stolen from Germany.

He had the paintings examined by an art expert, who confirmed authenticity. The expert was confused, however, by a spot of green paint for which he could not account. The collector explained, "The green paint comes from the man who painted my house. I told him to put a drop cloth over everything, but he didn't and the paint was splattered all around."

The collector became involved in a litigation with both the West and East German governments, who forcefully sought the return of the paintings both through courts and by diplomatic means. After a long and expensive legal battle, he had to return the paintings. But for 30 years, he had owned them and loved them.

There are other finds for you to make; maybe not quite so dramatic, but just as exciting. The key is to be informed. Take advantage of every opportunity to look.

A fine artist with whom I am personally acquainted studied with Reginald Marsh and Yasuo Kuniyoshi at New York's Art Student's League after World War II. One day, I mentioned to him that I owned some lithographs by Marsh, who is a favorite of mine. He began reminiscing about his days at school with Marsh and showed me some of his photographs and other memorabilia. "Wait," he said, "I have some sketches by Marsh. He would correct my work with sketches and watercolors, and I kept them."

My friend looked, but couldn't find them. I hope they're not lost. Someday, they'll turn up. Perphaps some art collector will be rooting through an attic and recognize what he finds... because if he's knowledgeable, when he sees it, he'll recognize what he has found.

Book and junk shops are also excellent sources of art. Like the attic, these shops have materials piled all over them. You never know what you're going to find, or where.

Some years ago, while driving through the Catskill mountains, I stopped at several old junk shops along the way. At one place, I notice a box of old prints. One of my collecting interests is New York City. I collect whatever I can find about it. And in this box, along with other things, I found an 1837 Valentine's print of the Narrows. (That's the body of water between Brooklyn and Staten Island, as you enter New York Harbor.) It was framed under glass. I bought it for $2. Frame and all.

Such a print, in New York City, in that condition, would have brought at least $75, unframed. Remember, the further you are geographically from the area of collection, the cheaper the price. Never be surprised to find any works of art in unusal places. They can come to you in all sorts of places, all over the world. Just exploit the fact that when you do find such a work, you may have a better idea of its value than the disinterested seller.

Antique shops are tricky. If you look in a high-priced quality antique shop, you probably won't find any lost treasures. You may even be overpaying for a cleaned-up canvas and fancy frame. The kind of antique shop that borders on being a junk shop, however, generally just stores stuff around. This kind of shop buys complete attic or estate contents, without going through each item, whereas a high priced antique shop carefully selects its purchases, grooms them, and is well aware of the value of everything it sells.

Let's return to auctions. Collectors at large have been buying more art at auctions within the past few years than ever before. Auctions are interesting, and because they are well publicized, they tend to establish the price for an artist's work or for an edition of a fine print.

Reputable international houses will do their best to authenticate the art they sell. You needn't attend an auction to bid. You may bid by mail or phone, directly from the catalogue.

There is a method to buying art at auctions, which I caution you to study carefully before you consider buying. You should first learn how to bid, or "offer," and know when there is an acceptance. Once the auctioneer accepts your bid as the highest, he bangs a gavel or makes some other gesture which seals the formal acceptance. At this point, you cannot withdraw your offer.

You must learn the terms that auctions houses use to authenticate and describe works for sale. Auction houses publish catalogues (which you should keep for further reference). As a prospective bidder you may, of course, make an inspection before the auction. Look at the print with its catalogue description in hand. Soon you will learn the condition of a work merely by its description.

When an auction house says a painting is "after" an artist, they are saying that the artist himself may not have painted the work, but that someone else, perhaps one of his students, has executed it in the painter's style.

There are terms used to describe an authentication of a painting which you must know before you begin to actively participate in bidding. Learn them. Auctions can be an excellent source of acquiring bargains. Before you get started, however, you must thoroughly understand the rules and the nomenclature.

Plate A: *Sixth Avenue II*, lithograph, Fairfield Porter.

Plate B: *Fishing Nets*, watercolor, Epifanio Irizarry.

Plate C: *Liberty*, mezzotint, Fred Mershimer.

Plate D: *Fire Call*, oil on board, Robert Riggs.

Plate E: *The Fortune Teller*, watercolor, William Schwartz.

Plate F: *View from Jacmel*, oil on board, Gilber Desir.

Plate G: *Concierge*, watercolor, Paul Sample.

Plate H: *Customs House*, oil on canvas, Maurice Grosser.

Plate #10: *Geisha*, woodblock, artist unknown.

CHAPTER IX
Esoteric Art

I use the term "Esoteric Art" to mean any art with which you have no familiarity. If you are collecting abstract art and have specialized in that area, you're going to find yourself on unfamiliar ground amongst primitive Haitian art, or Grandma Moses.

Admittedly, they are charming and colorful, but you've got to know what you are doing. After all, when you buy a painting, you're investing good money; money that could be used to fill out your collection. But if you have taken the trouble to understand and know what suits you, then when you come up against art styles that you know little or nothing about, you will proceed with caution. As I've said before, there is so much to learn about and know within any particular area of art, going far afield will sap your finances and dilute your collection.

If you travel, you will be exposed to art of many cultures. Japanese wood blocks, for instance, are lovely. But because the great Japanese masters neither numbered their blocks nor destroyed them, many current strikes are available. An expert in Japanese wood blocks can tell, by color and line, when the print was first pulled. That makes a difference in price. I'm not saying, "don't buy beautiful Japanese wood blocks because you don't know anything about that type of art." What I am saying is that the price of such a work is based upon so many complicated factors that only an expert can point them out to you. If you don't have an expert handy, beware.

The same is true of Persian or Indian art. Much of it is ceremonial. It may have a national or ceremonial meaning, which affects the price. Unless you understand these factors, you could get hurt.

You don't have to collect only one type of art. You can have

69

several areas of expertise and that will make collecting a lot more fun. Personally, I collect in more than one area. I collect New York City scenes, American artists of the 1930's and '40's, and maritime scenes. I tend to like representational or impressionistic artists, but that's my taste. You will have your own.

I've bought art that didn't fit into any of the categories I've mentioned, but it was always with an eye to understanding what the artist was doing, because he was painting in a style I knew and could enjoy. Recently, my tastes have moved toward more abstract designs, those in which form dissolves into shape, and where color is important. I've always been interesed in and tried to keep up on all forms of arts, whether they excite me or not. So my interest in this new style is, for me, a natural development. I'm now interested in art which I've always been aware of, if not ready to buy. It's sort of like changing neighborhoods and moving into a new house. You begin to see things differently.

This may happen to you. If it does, consider it a healthy development. Learn all about the new style in which you are interested, so that you can become just as proficient in collecting your new interest as you were with the old.

Plate #11: *Out*, lithograph, Robert Riggs.

CHAPTER X
Taking Care of What You've Bought

If you are an avid collector, in time you'll have a houseful of art. Bare walls will annoy you. You'll soon have no place to hang what you bought last. Then, the size of the painting will be a consideration in your purchase. If it's too large, there will be no place to hang it. Your collection will overflow into your office, the kitchen, and perhaps even the bathroom. If you are a collecting addict, you may even find yourself piling canvasses into the corner of a spare room.

You are the custodian of the art you have acquired. You are charged with the reponsibility of caring for it during your lifetime. If you've selected wisely, many things you've bought will be important and timeless, even if you don't think of them that way. They at least represent an investment to you of a considerable amount of money and time. For these reasons, you must take care of your art and make sure it doesn't deteriorate.

Museums around the world maintain their art collections with constant temperature and humidity control. This prevents paper and canvas from expanding, drying, or becoming moist.

Unfortunately, the cost of power puts this kind of perpetual care beyond the reach of most of us. We must learn other ways to keep our art in fine condition.

As we've seen, fine prints, watercolors and drawings are the most delicate works of arts. Executed on paper, they are subject to tearing, creasing, smudging from dirty hands and general soiling.

When purchasing fine prints or watercolors, make sure they have been executed on quality paper, such as Arches or Japan. That is a definite plus in the preservation of your acquisition. For example, some Arches paper intended for watercolor is of heavy durable quality. When handled, it makes a noise similar to thin sheet metal.

Of course, artists cannot always print or paint on that kind of paper. Delicate papers are often purposely used to carry out an airy theme. But you should know what kind of paper you are dealing with. I own watercolors painted during the Depression that were painted on brown paper. Extra care has to be taken for their preservation, because wrapping paper is not manufactured to last. It's thin, with short fibers, and subject to quick and early deterioration.

Let's start from the very beginning of your care program. If you are buying a print in a gallery, there may be four or five of the same edition available. Select the one that's in the best condition (don't forget your magnifying glass.) Handle the print with care. After you have made your selection, the gallery will put cardboard on both sides of your print for stability until you get it home. Handle your cargo carefully.

You may do one of two things with prints. They may be framed, or set up in a bin, unframed. The bin allows you to go through them from time to time, much as you would look at photographs. One of the advantages of prints is that they may be stored, if done properly, with relative ease when they're not framed.

If you decide to frame, use only a rag mat (also known as PH or Museum Board.) That is an absolute must! If any other type of mat comes in contact with your print, it will eventually cause a chemical reaction from the acids present in paper. Any other mat will discolor and deteriorate your prints.

Never, never, permit a framer to back a print with plain cardboard or wood. These will also make chemical contact with paper, which destroys its integrity. I have seen wood grains transferred to the back of a lovely print, destroying its value forever.

Many framers don't use rag mats unless you specifically request it. Rag mats are more expensive than regular mounting board, but you should consider nothing else.

Never asume that because you've bought a top quality work of art from a well-known dealer that it's properly framed. Dealers buy from individuals and often leave the works in the same frame to sell to you. If the work was improperly framed to begin with, that's how you'll get it from the gallery.

When your framer mounts a print, never permit him to paste the edges to the board. Paste dries, becomes lumpy and warps paper, making your print lose value. Insist that he hinge the piece to the mat, instead. Hinges are delicate tapes which are fixed to the back of your print and then to the mat in a hinge-like manner. It does away with pasting, and other damaging forms of fixing your print... to an extent. You will always have marks from the hinges, but they minimize direct contact, perserving the print as much as is possible.

Make sure that you put a print, watercolor or any other work of art executed on paper, beneath a mat. Framing without a mat means placing glass directly on to the work. This causes transfer; that is, pigment from the art will transfer directly to the glass, paper will stick to the glass, and humidity will cause the paper to warp. In any case, you can eventually throw the print out.

If you treasure what you have bought and want it to last, or are considering selling part or all of your collection in the future, the time spent with the framer, pointing out to him that you want your art to be protected, is essential. Pick a good framer and stick with him. He'll know and understand your needs.

While works on paper must be matted and placed beneath glass to protect them from the elements, acrylics, a recent development in art, may be treated as oils. Acrylics are plastic pigments which do not react or deteriorate as quickly as print pigments or watercolors. However, if you have an acrylic which is painted on paper in watercolor style, you should then treat it as you would a watercolor: place it beneath glass, both to protect the paper and to carry off the watercolor theme.

A word about glass. Glass both protects the art work and permits you to see through to it. Sometimes, glare or reflection in glass interferes with your visual enjoyment. Technology has developed a non-glare glass, which breaks light down, diffusing it, and reducing glare considerably.

Personally, I find it unsatisfactory because it also detracts from the brilliance of the colors on the other side. I have used non-glare glass occasionally and only once was completely satisfied. When you get a glare on a piece, you're probably better off moving it to a spot where you don't have reflection.

When you hang works of art, make sure the nails or hooks or whatever else you're using, are good and strong. You don't want a frame to come crashing down, breaking both glass and wood.

If your framer has done his job properly, he has sealed off the paper from the outside. A crack in the glass permits fungus, dirt and moisture to enter on to the paper. Soon, you will have little brown spots (foxing) or holes on your work, which will destroy its value. If you don't get that, you'll get collections of moisture which look like watermarks and are equally damaging.

Once I hung an engraving near an air conditioner. The cold air blew into the frame, which had a crack in the glass. When the air conditioner was off, warm moist air collected under the glass. After a few weeks of this hot-cold treatment, I noticed that a sheet of ice was collecting on the print! I changed the glass and moved the print, but alas, a water stain had permanently scarred the paper.

Periodically, check the corners or right angles of your frames to ensure that they are tight. The four corners of a frame are joints which are joined at right angles by the framer. As wood cures, it could cause separation from a joint with openings that permit the entry of dirt and moisture.

Check the back of the frame periodically as well. Framers use fairly thin paper, which they glue to the frame to seal it off. With time, it may dry up or become moist, depending on where you live. If it dries up, it will tear and expose the reverse side of your mat. If it becomes moist, it may transfer moisture to mat and paper.

Be careful where you hang your work. Should you hang it on a wall that has water pipes running through it (if you can avoid this,please do) put foam rubber bumpers on the back of the frame to prevent direct contact with the wall. Don't hang frames near moist areas either, such as fish tanks or steam radiators.

Light is another great enemy of works of art on paper and canvas. Since pigments on paper are more delicate than oils, they deteriorate quicker than an oil painting. Never hang a work of art where it will constantly be exposed to daily doses of sunlight. It will soon fade, lose its beauty, and become discolored. If you have no other choice, then hang a shade or drape on the window, to keep out the sun's rays.

If you have a valuable collection, you should consider other ways to constantly protect your art. Windows can be treated with a solar screen, which cuts down on the harmful effects of the sun's ultraviolet rays by as much as 92%, and keeps the house from overheating. It is expensive, but if the sun ruins one or two of your paintings, you might lose more than the cost of protection... and a lot more than what the painting might have sold for.

A good example of what I mean about damage occurring through inattention was when a friend invited me to his home to show me his Picasso print. It was a lovely piece, but it was discolored, showing signs of damage along the corners. It was disturbing to see a Picasso attacked by light and atmosphere for lack of proper basic care. The loss was in thousands of dollars. Simple care and the investment of only a few dollars could have avoided the problem.

Periodically, change the location of your paintings. Even if they aren't exposed to sunlight, they might be exposed to constant light from electric bulbs, flourescent lights, and the reflected glare from the outside. Moving them around prevents this constant assault. Again, keep your paintings away from very dry areas. Any extremes from the average temperature of your home can be harmful to your art.

A word of caution about pastels and charcoals. These are created by rubbing chalky or powdery substances on paper. Don't move them around unless absolutely necessary. Movement may rearrange the powdery film. If you are careless in your handling, you may find a country scene suddenly change into a free form abstract.

If you are not going to hang your prints, you should put them in a bin, in the same ways that galleries display them, or in a Solander box. A Solander box is especially designed to hold prints and keep them free from humidity. You can buy one in any art shop.

I have dozens of unframed prints and watercolors and no room to hang them. I have my own formula for care. As soon as I acquire a new one, I promptly mat it so it will stay stiff and straight. Then I cover it with plastic. In this way, I can handle it without concerning myself about the state of my hands. Nor do I worry about creasing or bending, because it is matted.

Canvas and oil also require special protection. Canvas is cloth and stretches just as your shirt or dress might. Dry oils can become brittle and crack. Oil breaks down when a canvas sags or stretches. Oils can also lose their brilliance with time. Every oil changes its tone immediately after it's been painted. Artists call it "mellowing." That's natural. But oil paintings can also get dirty and lose their lustre.

If you are considering buying an oil painted on board, make sure the board is not warped or cracked. It should be framed in such a way as to keep it from cracking. If an oil is painted on canvas it is attached to a stretcher. The stretches is what gives a canvas its shape. A stretcher is nothing more than four pieces of wood joined at right angles, to hold the canvas. It is very important that canvas be stretched properly. If it's too loose, the canvas will sag, causing ripples in the painting. If it's too tight, the canvas will pull and tear and the paint will crack. You will soon be able to look right through the paint on to the canvas.

If you're traveling,and buy an oil painting, always consider where you bought it in relation to where you live. If you've bought the painting in a warm, moist climate, the wood on the stretcher will be swollen with moisture. The stretcher will shrink and the canvas will sag when you get back home, if you live in a dry climate. If you live in a humid climate, and buy the painting in, say Arizona, where it is dry, your stretcher will swell up when you get it home, causing the canvas to become taut.

It would be well to consider restretching oils in such situations. Problems with stretchers don't happen right away, but you might regret not having changed a stretcher several months later. It might pay not to frame the painting for a while, but to leave it on the stretcher to see how it "settles in."

To illustrate how wood behaves, I've bought several wood carvings, only to have them develop little splits months later, because the wood was adjusting to a different climate.

Another word of caution. On a trip to warm tropical countries, you might want to buy some enchanting paintings already stretched and framed. Check the stretchers and frames carefully. They could have termites. Not only will termites ruin your painting, but they could spread to other wood furniture in your home. Be very careful.

Oils tends to collect dust, which should be removed periodically, because dust builds a film over your canvas, changing the brilliance of the color. Go very lightly over your oil paintings with a soft artist's brush on a regular basis. Artists, when painting, build up oils on parts of the canvas and you would not want to break them off or damage them in any way by using a cloth or feather duster.

Using the same soft brush, lightly clean the bottom of your painting, where the frame meets the canvas. Dust accumulates there through the force of gravity. You should do the same for framed prints. When dusting, always work from the top down.

If you are using a glass cleanser when cleaning a framed print, never put fluid in a corner near the frame. It may seep through to the print. Always put liquid glass cleanser on the center of the glass and work outwards with a cloth. Of course, you should hold the frame flat, at right angles to your stomach.

A word about restoration. With all your care and attention, you may find a piece has become damaged anyway. This may happen because the paper was not of good quality, or because the oils were not painted on a good undercoating, or for a variety of other reasons. Art restorers can perform wonders with damage. Don't wait. Repair immediately. Prints are restored by bathing them in certain solutions. Oils can be worked over. Consult your gallery or museum for expert care. The results can be miraculous.

Plate #12: *Bread Line*, woodcut, Claire Leighton.

CHAPTER XI
Insurance

If you have spent a great deal of money on your collection, you should think about insuring it. It's a personal decision. I insure my collection. You probably insure your camera, your coin or stamp collection, your jewelry. A painting should certainly get the same consideration.

Art insurance is relatively inexpensive. But there are some things you should know about insurance. Paintings will not be insured against fading from sunlight, or natural deterioration. Paintings can be insured against theft, fire, flood and other disasters. If you are interested, call your insurance broker and ask about a Fine Arts policy.

You should maintain a catalogue of every work you have bought, including such information as when you bought it, from whom and for how much. The insurance carrier, in order to determine your premium, must have some idea of how much the painting is worth. Your best proof is the bill of sale. Never lose it. Based on the prices paid, the insurance carrier will quote a premium for the insurance. If you feel the quote is high, go through your collection. I personally do not insure any work valued at less than $250. You should pick the amount for which you feel you can act as a self-insurer, and insure those works which are valued at a higher amount.

Over the years, your collection's value will increase. Increase your insurance accordingly. Remember when I asked you to hold on to those catalogues and bills? Here is where you will need them. To establish new values for your art, you can show current gallery or auction prices right from the catalogue. This should be enough to satisfy any insurance carrier.

Oils, watercolors and other one of a kind works may be more difficult to establish a value on, but you can always get an appraisal. In the past few years, I have watched many of my purchases increase in value by three to ten times their original cost. I photocopy the catalogues with the pictures of the works and their current value. Then I send them to my insurance broker with a request to increase coverage accordingly.

If anyone has made a legitimate, bona-fide offer, in writing, for one of your paintings, you could submit that as a current value. If you don't have such an offer, go to your bill of sale, or write the gallery where you purchased the work. Send them a letter such as this one:

Dear Sir:
I own an 18" x 20" painting by John Doe, executed in 1982, titled "Dawn." It's an oil on canvas, in good condition, purchased from your gallery in January 1985.

Would you please be so kind as to indicate what the present value of this painting would be? Please indicate same on the bottom of this letter, with your signature. I'm enclosing a return envelope for your convenience.

The gallery is probably still handling John Doe and is thus the best organization to appraise current value. If you've had good relations with the gallery, they should remember both you and the painting and be helpful with supplying the information. Some galleries might charge for such services, but the cost is well worth it. You can also get appraisals for a fee from auction houses and other art appraisers.

If you've collected some good works, and it is known around that you own certain pieces, you might some day get a call from a gallery, museum, or the artist, who are putting together an exhibit of retrospective works. "Would you allow us to exhibit artist John Doe's work, 'Dawn,' in Los Angeles?", they'll ask. It's flattering and you probably would allow it. However, before you let the painting go, determine who is to bear the cost of shipping and insurance while the painting is in transit and on exhibit.

If you move your home, check with the moving company and with your Fine Arts Policy to be sure your paintings are covered against damage while moving. If they are not, ask your mover to insure them. He will do this for an extra premium. Should you have any doubts, consult your insurance broker.

Plate #13: *Guts of the City*, lithograph, Louis Lozowick.

CHAPTER XII
Your Art and the Law

Laws governing the sale, delivery, and every other phase of art are just as applicable to you as they are to the purchaser of a Matisse who might spend half a million dollars for his treasure.

Your purchase is significant, even if you haven't bought a "name" artist or spent a lot of money. Galleries could not exist if they sold only important names like Matisse... or Dufy or Sloane or any of the old masters.

The same is true for auction houses. Million dollar sales draw publicity, and make big news, but average sales—and most collectors—will be in your category.

Let's start with the artist. He creates his dream on canvas and then puts it up for sale. When he sells it, does he give up all rights to it? Yes and No.

In Europe, an artist never loses his complete rights to his creation. This in known as "Droits Moral," (Moral Rights) and "Droit de Suite," (Right to Participate in Subsequent Sales).

The Droit Moral gives an European artist the rights (among others) to sue anyone who alters his work, and to refuse exhibition of his work unless he gets proper credit.

The Droit de Suite gives an artist participation in any increase in value of the work upon resale.

In recent years, American artists have been trying to get these rights through the courts. In fact, California has already passed such a law. It poses problems, but an artist may, when he sells you a painting, make such a contract with you. He may, for that matter, further restrict your ownership, as long as you both agree to it. For instance, an artist may copyright his painting: You cannot then reproduce it without his permission. I own such works, with copyright marks on their backs.

If an artist does not copyright his work, he may still maintain what is known as a "commonlaw copyright." What this means is that as long as the work remains private,no one can reproduce it without the artist's permission. Should it be widely exhibited, then the artist may lose his common law copyright. My advice to you, if you wish to reproduce a work you own, is to get permission from the artist or his estate. Copyright law is highly specialized and complicated and having the artist's permission can avoid future problems.

Many state have recently enacted laws to protect purchasers of art. Depending on the state (and you should check to see if your state has such a law), the gallery must list the number of prints or a description of the painting and its seller. By doing so, the seller guarantees an edition, or the authenticity of a painting. If the purchaser discovers that representation of the bill of sale is not true he may return the work and recover the purchase price (another reason to hold on to your sales receipts.)

Some states obligate the seller to make an actual representation of the numbers of fine prints in an edition or, in the alternative, a positive statement that the seller does not know the number of the edition.

Works bought at auctions have their own legal problems. Auctions use special language to which you are legally held. Auctioneers may withdraw a piece at any time, for any reason, unless stated otherwise. When an auction house lists a piece for sale, it uses certain descriptions to indicate what it feels the truth is about its authenticity. It is absolutely essential that you understand the code, since you may unwittingly buy something which is not authentic.

Any time an auction house warrants the authenticity of a piece, either by catalogue or through its employees, it will be held responsible to the truth of the warranty.

Remember, in purchasing prints or other art from an auction house, you have the right of inspection before the actual bidding time. Catalogue descriptions of the condition of the piece you are interested in should also be carefully noted. Get to know what the real condition of an object is by the special descriptions used by auction houses. While inspecting what interests you, take the time to look carefully at other works, too, even if you don't want to buy them. In the future, you will understand what those descriptions mean.

If you are interested in a piece, note its actual condition. You are charged with knowledge of an obvious defect on a piece when it is sold to you.

What happens when you buy a forgery or a fake? Well, again it depends on what representations were made to you. If your bill of sale reads, "'Dawn' by John Doe, 1982," then the dealer has represented to you that John Doe is the creator of the canvas.

When you purchase any work of art, be certain that the title of the painting, the medium, and the artist's name is on the bill of sale, like this:

Sold to Roland Smith, "Twilight," Serigraph, 31/75 by John Doe. Total edition 75, A/P 4.

This way, the gallery is making it very clear what you are buying. Don't hesitate to ask a dealer to put down anything else you may want on the bill of sale, such as the date executed, or the name of the printing workshop. After all, you are spending good money and you are entitled to such guarantees as you think you need. If a dealer wants to make a sale, he will comply. If he does not know, he will tell you. He certainly won't guarantee what he doesn't know.

Once you have warranties, you can come back for recovery of the purchase price should there be any breach. The dealer is aware of the law and won't put himself in any tough spots if he has doubts.

A while back, I bought 22 engravings of a certain artist over a two-year period. The artist is still alive, and owns the plates. When there is a call for his work, he prints them himself. None of the engravings are numbered, except to say "edition 100," and the dealer would not guarantee them on a bill of sale.

The dealer told me that it was well known that the artist would not print more than 100 of any edition. I bought them for several reasons. I know the dealer; he has a national reputation for integrity. Rather than make a sale, he would say that he didn't know. I did not know the artist personally, but from my inquiries I determined that he, too, has a good reputation. And finally, I wanted the engravings to fill out my collection. I took what I believed to be an informed risk.

After you get to know reputations and dealers, and want to add to your collection, you may find yourself in the same situation. What you will do then depends upon the information you are able to gather. By the way, some of those engravings have increased over a decade by as much as $900 a print.

In any event, remember that everything not warranted by the dealer on your bill of sale, leaves you vulnerable. Always try to get as much of the history of the piece as possible. Aside from the legal guarantees, the more you know about your works, the more saleable they will become, should you decide to sell them in the future.

Plate #14: *Friday on Orchard Street*, woodcut, Lou Barlow.

CHAPTER XIII
Art and Profits

Although my original concept for this book was to concentrate on the esthetics of art collecting rather than its investment value, some recent events in the world of art and its economics cannot be ignored. These are, of course, the auctions of important paintings which have been fetching millions of dollars.

The publicity given to these events attracts new people to art, arousing their interest as it shows art in a different way. Art becomes important because it carries a big dollar tag. It is the subject of conversation; it is "in" to collect expensive art.

When top level art values increase, I believe it creates a tide for other works of quality. People are attracted to collecting when they see prices doubling and tripling. Not everyone can collect million dollar masters such as Van Gogh, Rembrandt or Degas, so the rest of us become active within our budgets. It's a ripple effect—make a splash with the big paintings and the ripples travel all the way to the edge of the pond.

Understanding what works of quality are, collectors will seek them, creating a demand that pushes prices up on all art. Quality art is like gold or silver, always retaining its worth. So it is important you learn how to collect, not to grope. Seek the best and acquire it.

From the time the first germ of an idea came to me to write this book, until now, about 90% of my collection has appreciated substantially. Hardly two weeks go by without my receiving a catalogue or brochure for an exhibit describing works I've acquired years earlier. Usually the prices have risen dramatically.

The works of one artist, Armin Landeck, have rocketed 10 to 50 times in value over the prices I paid in 1974. And all indications are that Landeck's work will continue to climb.

An average increase for the rest of my art work is about 20 times above original purchase price. And during all this time, I've had the pleasure of having them around me. What kind of value do you place on that?

I have never consciously bought art as investment, but I always bought the best I could find and afford (even at times what I couldn't afford.) I was lucky to buy at low prices since I bought art that was then unfashionable. I knew it was good and that was all that mattered to me.

That art, now generally recognized as good and collectible, increased in value. But all quality works are increasing in value, because people are collecting everything that's good in every style and because today there are more serious collectors than ever before, and there is just so much art to buy.

I've been told by dealers recently that works I was collecting years ago are no longer generally available. As recently as 6 years ago you could find whatever you liked in that genre. When I bought my copy of a print it probably hadn't seen the light of day for 30 or 40 years. The prints were as pristine as the day they were struck decades earlier.

But today, because of the demand of the last few years, these works command up to $3,500 for a print I could have acquired for $600 just a few years ago. On the other hand, of course, those prints I did buy years ago are worth that much more, too.

It's important you understand these trends. As a new collector, you must take them into account. It's true that art is more valuable today than it was 25 years ago, but so are the incomes and cash available to the average family. But there are always new artists whose work can be obtained reasonably by discernible collectors. Then, you can sit back and watch its value grow.

Somewhere along the life of your collection, you will discover that the piece you bought a while back is worth a lot more than what you paid for it. What to do? You could sit back and admire it, taking pleasure in having been so clever and astute to have purchased it in the first place. But since this chapter is concerned with profits, I'm assuming you will sell the work.

Unless you've made a special arrangement with the artist, such as we've talked about earlier, you can sell it back to the gallery where you bought, sell it to an individual, or go to an auction house to have them put it up for sale.

The most obvious place to make the sale is to go back where you bought the piece and ask them to find a buyer. If it's a gallery, you'll probably have to pay a commission, which you should agree to in writing. This agreement should also include some other terms. For example, if the dealer hasn't sold the painting within a certain time period you may take it back free of any gallery charges. The gallery might make another arrangement with you: it might take back the painting and give you credit toward another purchase.

You might go to an auction house. In that case, remember that you'll have to pay a percentage of the sale as commission. Also, works of art tend to sell for less at auctions than at a gallery. Be careful: if you won't part with the piece for less than a certain amount, let the auctioneer know. He'll remove it from the bidding if he can't get your price.

If you are at the stage where you are personally acquainted with other collectors, you might ask if anyone else is interested. You might also check some of the art newsletters, to see if anyone is interested in the piece, or you might insert an ad yourself. But before you go hawking, you must establish actual value. If you've been holding on to newsletters and catalogues, you will be able to reconstruct the value of what you're selling. Once you've set value, you'll hold firm within a range. Good luck!

You might also consider donating the painting to a qualified charitable or tax deductible organization. As a collector, you may get the best advantage from a charitable donation. The role of the art donator has changed since the 1986 amended tax laws. There is a lot of confusion as to what you may actually deduct. My suggestion is this: if you plan to make a charitable donation of art works which have appreciated since you purchased them, consult with a qualified tax expert who can guide you properly.

Make sure the organization to which you make your donation qualifies as a charitable or tax deductible organization. Verify, too, that they can receive the painting in their charitable capacity. Sometimes, you may have a problem showing that the organization is using the art work in such a capacity. Before you make the donation, consult with your accountant to ensure that you are receiving maximum benefits for your donation, and that it is made properly.

A word about areas of collection vis-a-vis profit. This is a very risky situation. Don't collect only with an eye towards making a profit. It's tricky, like the stock market. You don't control flow, the big boys do. The key is to like what you're collecting, and always to try to collect quality. In this way, you can never go wrong.

The most important thing is to collect. Get out to the galleries and collect. Meet the artists and collect. Learn who other collectors are; go to the antique shops, search out attics, visit museums, read art magazines, and collect.

You will have the same joys and pleasures I have experienced in the art world in the last 25 years.

Plate #15: *Brooklyn Brigde*, engraving, Fred Mershimer.

CHAPTER XIV

About the Pictures in this Book

All the artwork in this book is part of my personal collection. Each was chosen to illustrate some element of art collecting. I'd like to share with you what I learned from these pictures... and how I feel about them. I purposely omitted presenting familiar works of art by the Masters, since they are generally available to you in art books and museums.

Cover: *Night Welder*, watercolor by Emil Trick

Unlike most artists represented in my collection, Emil Trick is not well known. It was at a street fair in New York City that I came upon the booth he and his wife tended. I liked everything he was showing. To me, his work illustrated the collector's wish to acquire works that purely attract the eye: there was no consideration of future value.

Trick's watercolors of New York City were spread out on his exhibition table and included scenes such as Wall Street, the Brooklyn Bridge, the New York Public Library, and more. I bought them all. *Night Welder* is my favorite. It has hung in my office for 15 years, and shares a wall with such well-known artists as Fritz Eichenberg, Howard Cook, Richard Haas and Claire Leighton. Visitors to my office are attracted by the charm of this little watercolor.

When I bought all of Trick's New York City scenes that day at the fair over 15 years ago, I paid an average of $8 each for more than a dozen watercolors. I've had offers to sell *Night Welder*, and refused them all.

I selected *Night Welder* as the cover of this book to

emphasize the collector's quest for art that pleases without necessarily costing a lot. What attracts many people to this work is the contrast of light and dark. Trick has also managed to pack a New York City skyline, a half-finished building, and a solitary welder kneeling on a girder amid a splash of sparks, within a small 6" x 8" image area. The impact is there. The picture has drama, contrast, solitude and New York's grandeur within very little space.

Plate #1
Cat's Paw, engraving by Armin Landeck

After about 7 years of serious collecting, I stumbled upon Armin Landeck. His work became the cornerstone of my collection: city spaces; familiar scenes of New York buildings, street corners and avenues I had grown up with. And the prints were all executed in the 1930's, '40's and '50's. When I first saw the pieces, I couldn't believe my eyes.

During the early 1970's, you could buy an exquisitely done Landeck for $45 to $70. Over the next 8 years, I bought over 35 Landeck's, ranging in price from $45 to a high of $300. When others began to recognize his talent, Landeck's prices began a steady rise. Today, the least expensive price for his work that I know of starts at $500 or $600 and moves into the thousands.

Again, Landeck fits the pattern of many artists in my collection. Well known during the '30's, '40's and '50's, he faded thereafter with the rise of abstract art, until tastes again changed in the 1970's. By then, he was printing his own work and filling many orders.

Landecks' work has been compared to Hopper's, in its quiet mood of silent streets and buildings. Landeck evokes his mood by portraying his city in a special way. Buildings speak, and empty streets beg you to walk them. Then, there are the rooftops. Landeck portrayed the tops of New York City's roofs as no one I know has ever done. The execution is precise, yet each chimney, eave, pipe and parapet has its own personality, separating it from every other building in New York City.

Cat's Paw is not a typical Landeck, but his unmistakeable talent can be seen in this execution. I've included it because there is genuine emotion in the lone doorman outside the

98

theatre, which the artist was later able to portray without putting people into his pictures. *Cat's Paw* was done in 1934.

Plate #2
Young Man, charcoal by Robert Riggs

Riggs was recognized as one of America's finest illustrators during the 1930's and '40's. His *Clown Alley* won prizes at the 1939 World's Fair. He was both a commercial and a fine artist, but then fell into an eclipse and was forgotten when abstract artists were in vogue.

During the late 1960's, Philip Desind of Capricorn Galleries in Bethesda, Maryland, acquired many of Riggs' works directly from the artist, who by then was living in obscurity in Philadelphia. Desind began exhibiting Riggs' work. He sincerely felt that Riggs deserved to be more widely appreciated. At first, the works sold at low prices. Before long, Riggs was rediscovered, and his work was in high demand. Today, Riggs' works are in the same class as many well-known American artists and sell for thousands of dollars.

I included this piece to illustrate an interesting point. *Young Man* is framed in non-glare glass. The most striking feature is the face. When our photographer, Selwyn Rosen, was photographing the picture, the bright studio lights again brought out many feature of this picture which I had not seen since I was originally attracted to it: Riggs' rich patterns in the suit jacket, the buttons and the face. I mention this to show that non-glare glass can sometimes reduce your enjoyment of a picture.

Riggs drew a companion piece to *Young Man* called *Young Woman*. *Young Woman* is still owned by Philip Desind and is part of his outstanding collection of American artists. The best of his collection is on loan to the Butler Institute in Ohio.

Plate #3
Whirpool, engraving by Charles McNulty

A lot of good artists have done interesting studies of Manhattan's skyline. This one is unusual because it draws you down from the skyline to look into the canyons formed by skyscrapers instead of looking up at or across their tops.

McNulty spread his buildings apart at physically impossible angles so that realistically drawn buildings are pitched at crazy slants. The result is a bit unsettling. Which is exactly the way McNulty wanted you to feel.

Plate #4

The Woolworth Through the Arch, engraving by Joseph Pennell

Sometimes, besides loving a work of art, I become aware and influenced by its history or the background of the artist. Works by Joseph Pennell fall into that category.

Pennell was born in Philadelphia in 1857 and died in 1926. During his lifetime, he was a well-known artist, concentrating on engravings such as *Woolworth*.

Pennell was fascinated with cities and machines. While living in England, he became a friend of James Whistler. Indeed, Whistler's influence can be seen in his work. Pennell owned many of Whistler's prints, which he eventually gave to the Library of Congress.

When Pennell returned to the United States, he led a full life... painting, teaching, lecturing, etc., and received many honors for his work.

He taught at the Art Students' League in New York, and many well-known American artists studied with him. So Pennell was the bridge between that giant expatriate American, Whistler, and students who would go on to become well known in their own right. A wheel come full circle.

I'm always puzzled that considering Pennell's background and talent, and the fact that most of his works are over 70 years old, they are still generally available at very reasonable prices.

The Woolworth Through the Arch was executed in 1921.

Plate #5

Central Park Night, lithograph by Adolf Dehnn

Dehn was the great producer of lithographs in America for a long time. Although well known for his series of New Yorkers, and night club and theatre performers, he, too, was generally limited in appeal. Recently Dehn's works have become widely circulated. Again, these works were, until recently, relatively reasonable in price but have increased to realistic values.

Central Park Night, executed in 1934, is for me the epitome of New York. Dehn has Central Park, the Manhattan skyline at Central Park South, and the blazing lights of unseen streets below reflecting the lower halves of the high towers. It gets you wondering about the kind of activity that can cause such a glow. With all that drama, Dehn takes the lower third of his image and transports you to a quiet, peopleless Central Park, dark save for a few lamplights.

Dehn never tired of portraying Central Park. I have one he did 30 years later, in color, with happy people enjoying the snow around the lake. And looming in the background are the towers of Manhattan.

Plate #6

Trio at Luchow's, oil on board by Frank Ashley

The theme of three musicans in art is a recurring one. Many artists have worked and developed it over the centuries. The most famous is Picasso's.

One of the first posters to hang in my home while I was still a student at law school, was Picasso's rendition. I loved the colors and the composition; the cubist form. Later I learned that Picasso made more than one version of his Three Musicians.

Ashley's rendition attracted me because the musicians were not just posing for a portrait. These men could be on a break, cigarette in hand and talking about matters unassociated with music. They are alive and I often feel when I look at this painting that I am interrupting their conversation.

Plate #7

Greetings from the Wehye, woodcut by Howard Cook

Cook, a fine print graphic artist who recently died, was well known from the 1930's through the present. He did this woodcut as a greeting card for the Wehye Gallery in New York City in 1929. The Weyhe was then famous as a gathering place for artists and writers, and it was portrayed by other artists during this period.

Both my wife and I love this print. It reminds us of the many hours we've spent at the Wehye, which still does business on Lexington Avenue. The art gallery is on the second floor, over a book shop at street level. It is a mother lode of old prints. We can never leave the Wehye without taking something with us including, on one occasion, this Cook print.

Cook, within a smaller surface than Trick (4¼" x 7 ½"), also manages to pack contrast, drama, skyline and activity into his image. The reason I included Cook's print in this book is to show how all these things can be achieved without color.

Plate #8
El Conde, pencil sketch on paper by Samuel Lind
We go to Samuel Lind's workshop often. He is a pleasant young man with a gift for rendering colors so bright they seem to glow in daylight. Lind's work is so popular that there is barely anything available for sale in his studio. He often works on commission, doing murals for an office building or a bank or posters for festivals.

Once, he was working on a huge, happy canvas, depicting a rural scene of people dancing at a festival. The scene was full of action and color. On another side of his large work area, there were pencil sketches of individual figures in that oil painting. I purchased two sketches; *El Conde* is one of them. While the sketch is not in color, the essence of action is there.

El Conde, attracted me because of the execution of the lone dancer. Hands extended to emphasize his position, he is for me the eternal, graceful dancer who strives to please his audience with elegant movements.

Plate #9
Erie R.R. Yards, lithograph by Reginald Marsh
One of the great interpreters of urban America, Reginald Marsh was born to a comfortable family, studied in Paris, then returned to America to paint tatoo parlors, sailors, drunks, burlesque halls, and down and outers. He belonged to the "Ashcan School" of American art which was derided because of their insistence in showing the seamy side of American cities during the early part of this century.

In a Marsh painting, the women are Reubenesque, fleshy and thick-thighed, but always independent, gay and aware of the world around them. His sailors are ever on the make and his drunks are a chronicle of the old Bowery, when the Third Avenue El clattered overhead and forgotten men hid in the shadows below.

Marsh's paintings are always alive with color and light, rarely depressing and filled with urban activity such as the clutter of signs, striped barber poles, signs of tatoo parlors and people interacting on city streets.

Erie R.R. Yards show Marsh's treatment of the working man. The workers appear to be leaving their jobs after a day's work and are bent and weary. The only person standing straight is the man in the shack, who is a fellow worker but obviously has not put in the same kind of working day.

That Marsh cared for and loved his city people is obvious in any of his works.

Plate #10
Geisha, woodblock, artist unknown.

Japanese woodblocks are a familiar form of art. They are characterized by flat, two-dimensional shapes, usually very decorative with bright colors. Unlike primitive art, figures are properly proportioned to each other and are well drawn. There is an air of elegance about the execution, which is often complicated.

I've included this woodblock as an illustration of one form of art among the many I'd like you to look at. It is also interesting to know that Japanese woodblock has made an impact upon Western art.

French Impressionists during the late 19th century became intrigued with the Japanese woodblock designs on the tissue paper then used to wrap products which had come to Paris from the Orient. Artists like Whistler, Mary Cassat, Degas, Gaugin and even Van Gogh incorporated Japanese techniques onto their canvases and prints. Some of the posters of that time also show definite influence of this Japanese art form. All of which proves that artists from different cultures have much to learn from each other.

Plate #11
Out, lithograph by Robert Riggs

Riggs' talent ran from oils and drawings to graphics. This litograph is one of a series of boxing scenes done by Riggs at the height of his career.

Out is included to show how emotions can be garnered, not only by color or contrast, but by skillful artwork in portraying facial expressions. The work also points out that a fine talent such as Riggs' can be expressed in more than one medium.

Plate #12

Bread Line, N.Y., woodcut by Claire Leighton

Claire Leighton is well known for woodcuts. Usually the scenes are rural fields and country scenes. *Bread Line, N.Y.* was done in 1934 during the depths of the Depression.

Leighton's interesting use of the vanishing point and perspective has always fascinated me. While using representational forms, the vanishing point is created by the union of four lines. Then Leighton divides the image within four segments: skyscrapers, an elevated train, a white strip of thoroughfare and the breadline itself, creating a fifth subsidiary line as the long line of men disappears into the vanishing point.

It's almost cubistic, since while all divisions fit into the theme or idea, they logically don't fit into the sections of the print assigned to them.

With the men in the foreground warming themselves over a winter fire, executed in black and white, *Breadline, N.Y.* is a powerful reminder of hardships suffered by Americans during the 1930's. Leighton's print qualifies as a fine example of art commenting on social conditions.

Plate #13

Guts of the City, lithograph by Louis Lozowick

Another well known chronicler of urban America, Louis Lozowick's works are precise, almost mathematical as when he has sunlight peeping through the tracks of an elevated train, making orderly patterns on the street below. Yet Lozowick is not cold or aloof. He fills his images with people doing every day tasks, working, and carrying on with their lives.

In *Guts of the City*, two workers are below street level (you can see the wheel of a car at the top of the picture.) They are engaged in repairing some part of the vast, hidden support system which keeps any city alive.

Look closely: you can see Lozowick's statement. Here are the city's arteries, her organs. Perhaps that big tank could be her lungs or even her heart. You can almost sense blood flowing through the heavy hoses. And above the workers is the skin covering the city's vitals.

Plate #14

Friday on Orchard Street, woodcut by Lou Barlow

During the Depression, the U.S. government underwrote many artistic projects. Artists were hired to create murals in the lobbies of post offices and other federal office buildings. America's great artists, such as Ben Shahn, Reginald Marsh and Thomas Hart Benton created marvelous works during this period. If you are near such buildings, you should see these works, as they are usually done on a grand scale, covering large areas of public hallways and rotundas.

Lew Barlow's *Friday on Orchard Street* was created for the Federal Art Project of the W.P.A., the same agency that commissioned the large works. Many artists created canvases, sculpture and prints for the W.P.A., ususally depicting some facet of American life or history.

Barlow has captured the Lower East Side ritual of buying fish on Friday to use for supper on the Jewish sabbath. I don't know when this woodblock was executed, but the price of the fish could be a clue.

Plate #15

Brooklyn Bridge, engraving by Frederick Mershimer

If you've had the pleasure of seeing the Brooklyn Bridge up close, you couldn't help but fall in love with her. While at law school, I walked the bridge at least twice a week over a three year period.

Remaining with me through the years since, are her two most exciting features: the Gothic shape of her towers, which arch to points much like the great, stone interiors of medieval churches, and the exquisite webbing of her cables, spider fine, surrounding the towers like a protective net.

I own many pictures of the Brooklyn Bridge, and each

reminds me of a different way in which I've seen her. This version comes closest to the way I think of her... a great, stone monument to American progress.

COLOR PLATES

Plate A
Sixth Avenue II, lithograph by Fairfield Porter

Fairfield Porter is an example of what I've been saying in this book. He was one of America's finest artists, but as a representational painter, he received recognition from a relatively small group of art lovers, critics and collectors.

Within the last few years, he was "rediscovered" and his works exhibited in Boston, New York and elsewhere. Prices for his works have soared.

Sixth Avenue II shows Sixth Avenue at Greenwich Village looking North. Porter portrays the essence of moving traffic on a heavily travelled Manhattan street. He also captures a grey New York day, where all colors seem to tone down and almost become one.

This picture hangs on a wall by my desk so that when I'm on the telephone I'm usually looking at it. When I do, traffic moves, the wash of wheels and motors floats over the city and I remember the heady smells of Greenwich Village.

Look at the pink building above the truck on the right side of the picture. Do you see Porter's initials? Putting in initials, triangles, boxes and rectangles are a time honored device used by artists. Sometimes they are used to make the painting interesting. Sometimes an artist will include a shape to draw your attention to something he wants you to see nearby.

Next time you have the opportunity to look at paintings in a museum, see how some artists use letters and shapes to perk up your interest.

Plate B
Fishing Nets, watercolor by Epifanio Irizarry

Fishing Nets is an example of abstraction. Irizarry has created a filmy area arcing into points along its upper edges. The points are the heads and bodies of fishermen who are straining to pull on a large net. They are there and they aren't. The net is there and it isn't. When I look at paintings like this, I think of Debussy's music: soft, dreamy, susceptible to lots of personal meanings and ideas.

Sometimes, Irizarry will wash his watercolors with a sopping sponge to loosen up the subject. It literally flows and the original hardness disappears into a soft gauzy haze. Art of this type holds different meanings for different observers. You are important as the viewer to give the canvas its meaning and life. I've seen Irizarry take subjects with a hard edge and dissolve them into colors flowing into each other.

When you become friendly with the artists and visit their studios, you learn much about techniques and can more readily appreciate the talent that flows from a brush or engraving tool onto canvas or paper.

Plate C
Liberty, engraving by Fred Mershimer
I've included Mershimer's work for two reasons. The first is the obvious quality of craftmanship, the impact of light and dark, color, composition and drama. *Liberty* is a striking piece of work.

Handled improperly, this work could have turned out trite. Instead, it is a fresh and original look at a familiar American symbol.

For new collectors who think works of good artists have already been scooped up and are out of reach, think of Mershimer. He is a young printmaker with a bright future. We learned about him simply because we are always on the alert for works of quality regardless of the artist's eminence. My wife saw his work at the Newmark Gallery in New York, liked the piece she saw, bought it on the spot and then learned that Mershimer worked at the Gallery's framing deparment. We have a standing order to buy every piece he does, as soon as they are completed.

Plate D
Fire Call, oil by Robert Riggs
While Riggs was known as an illustrator and a Realist, he had a natural sense for movement bordering on the abstract. If you squint your eyes, you can see how he placed movement

across the canvas, portraying the feeling of urgent action. One really gets the feeling of excitement and speed.

The police officers on the truck, almost in silhouette, their arms flailing, are outlined against the garage wall. A woman and boy both look amazed at the activity surrounding them. A directing officer jumps to life between the civilians and the officers, pulling both parts of the painting together and at the same time separating the observers from participants.

Fire Call is a perfect example of Riggs' talent. This oil, together with several others, was painted for a national magazine as illustrations for a piece about the New York City Police Department. After 40 years, this painting holds up, separate and apart from its original commercial theme, as a fine work of art.

Plate E
The Fortune Teller, watercolor by William Schwartz

Fantasy wrapped up in realistic trappings. Just look at the walls. They don't make right angles where they meet. The chairs are out of proportion, so are the tables, as well as the people sitting beside the fortune teller.

At first glance, this picture looks somewhat real. But the closer one looks, the more amazing it becomes. No two people see this painting the same way. For instance, the picture on the wall, to me, has always depicted the madonna and child. I usually get arguments on that one. See the window? Are those curtains billowing through or a fat lady's legs?

I like to think of this picture as the thinking man's art. No matter how often I look I always see something new. The colors add to my pleasure of this wonderful painting, as do the odd designs on the walls and the flowers.

Besides being an accomplished artist, William Schwartz sang for the Chicago opera.

Plate F
View from Jacmel, oil on board by Gilbert Desir

Haiti has long been associated with primitive art. *View from Jacmel* is a good example of what has been called primitive, naive, or native art. This kind of art is usually associated with bright colors, lack of perspective and lack of interrelationship between subjects with no depth or dimension to the figures. Note Desir's outsized people in relation to the houses and the street. It is charming, I think, basically because it reminds us of youngsters at work.

There have been many famous painters in the style of the primitives: Rousseau, who painted with the Impressionists; Grandma Moses; and Moses of Safed are some that come to mind.

At one time, Haitian painters were almost exclusively using this style. Many Haitians now study abroad and paint in different styles. If naive art appeals to you, consider Haitian art, because reasonably priced canvases are abundant.

Beware, however. Once you get to know Haitian art, you will quickly learn that for each master there are a dozen skillful copiers. On my first art trip to Haiti 16 years ago, I allowed a travelling companion to have first choice of some art we both liked. When the gallery owner noted my disappointment at not being able to purchase one piece in particular, he said, "Come back in two hours; I'll have another one for you."

The owner was true to his word. Two hours later, he sold me a similar canvas, still smelling of oil paint.

Later, I learned much about Haitian art, made frequent trips to the island and bought many paintings to sell to clients. As close as I was to so many of the paintings, and as charmed as I am by them and the technique of Haitian paintings, I do not collect them in large numbers. I know several people who collect nothing but primitive art, however, and that is right for them.

Plate G
Concierge, watercolor by Paul Sample

Sample was a virtuoso at watercolors. This early work shows the promise of the fine artist that was to be. Sample's oils were always large in scope, usually portraying outdoor scenes such as ships passing up a river or wide valleys.

In later life, Sample became Artist in Residence at Dartmouth College in New Hampshire. He executed many watercolors of snow laden fields with slashes of blue river across the image. There are elements of the abstract in these paintings when seen from a distance. The whiteness of the snow cut by deep blue creates dramatic and pleasing pictures.

Plate H
Customs House, oil on canvas by Maurice Grosser

Besides being a fine artist, Grosser was an accomplished writer. He served as art critic for the old *Saturday Review* and wrote about his life as a painter in a book called *Painter's Progress.*

Grosser studied art in Paris with Impressionists. He ground his own pigments, made his own canvas and generally prepared his own materials much as early painters did before manufactured materials were available.

In *Painter's Progress*, Grosser tells how, because of inexperience in preparation, some of his paints and canvases deteriorated. Luckily, *Customs House* is still intact.

Note how Grosser positions squares and rectangles to create the Customs House; almost like building blocks. Especially pleasing to me is his recreation of reflections in the water.

This painting was one of a series he executed of scenes of the Mediterranean.

BIBLIOGRAPHY

It is impossible, in a book of this size, to point out every-thing a collector needs to know. Although not much has been written about collecting per se, there is a lot of literature covering individual aspects of art. I've put together a biblio-graphy which should give you a clear picture of the field of art and art collecting as it stands today.

In compiling this book list, I've assumed that you will be concentrating on American artists, so included are books that will be helpful in that area. I've covered the field generally, and leave it to you to further research the individual artists and styles which appeal to you.

I. How to Look at Art

Gaunt, Williams and Harry N. Abrahams. *A Guide to the Understanding of Painting.*
Gombrich, E.H. *Art and Illusion.* Princeton Univ. Press,1972.
Grosser, Maurice. *Painter's Progress.* Clarkson W. Potter,1971.
Piper, David. Ed. *Enjoying Paintings.* Penguin Books, 1964.
Taylor, Joshua C. *Learning to Look: A Handbook for the Visual Arts.* University of Chicago Press, 1964.
Wolfflin, Heinrich. *Principals of Art History.* Dover Publi-cations, 6th ed., 1964.

II. Prints: Selection and Care

Eppink, Norman R. *101 Prints: The History and Techniques of Printmaking.* Univ. of Oklahoma Press, 1971.
Ivins, W.M., Jr. *How Prints Look.* Beacon Press, 1958.
Zigrosser & Gaehde. *A Guide to the Collecting and Care of Original Prints.*

III. Caring for your Artwork

Stout, George L. *The Care of Pictures.* Dover Publications, 1975.

IV. The Law and Art

Feldman and Weil. *Art Works, Law Policy.* Practicing Law Institute, 1974.

V. General Reference Works

Albers, Josef. *Interaction of Color.* ppbk. Yale University, 1975.
Batterbury, Michael. *Twentieth Century Art.* McGraw Hill Book Co., 1973.
Bull, George. *Vasari: The Lives of the Artists.* Penguin, 1972.
Cheney, Sheldon. *A Primer of Modern Art.* Liveright Publishing Corp., 1966.
Edwards, Betty. *Drawing on the Artist Within.* ppbk. Simon & Schuster, 1986.
Greenhill, Eleanor S. *Dictionary of Art.* Dell Publishing Co., 1974.
Malins, Frederick. *Understanding Paints: The Elements of Composition.* ppkb. Prentice Hall, 1981.
Prohaska, Ray. *A Basic Course in Design.* ppbk, North Light Publishers, 1980.

VI. Publications

Art Gallery Int'l
1224 East 17 Place
Tulsa, Oklahoma 74120

Art in America

Art News
P.O. Box 969
Farmingdale, New York 11737

The Artist's Magazine

P.O. Box 1999
Marion, Ohio 43305

The Print Collector's Newsletter
205 East 78th Street
New York, New York 10021

Pictures on Exhibit
30 East 60th Street
New York, New York

INDEX

Do You Have Questions?

Harry A. Ezratty, author of "How to Collect and Protect Works of Art," will answer individual questions about art. Write to him at P.O. Box 222, Stevensville, Md. 21666. Please send a stamped, self-addressed envelope for his response.

HARRY A. EZRATTY
Consultant
CORPORATE ART ACQUISITIONS

Harry A. Ezratty can ease your firm's entry into a corporate art acquisition program. To arrange for a consultation, use the form below.

———————————————————————————————————

TO: Harry A. Ezratty, Esq.
    P.O. Box 222
    Stevensville, Md. 21666

Yes, our company is interested in acquiring works of art. Please call us.

Name: _____

Position: _____ Tele: _____

Company: _____

Address: _____

_____